To Tim

From Mom + Dad
　　　Dec. 25 / 86

WHERE CHRIST IS STILL TORTURED

D0573545

Other books by Richard Wurmbrand

Answer to Moscow's Bible
If Prison Walls Could Speak
In God's Underground
Tortured for Christ

WHERE CHRIST IS STILL TORTURED

Richard Wurmbrand

Marshalls

Marshalls Paperbacks
Marshall Morgan & Scott
1 Bath Street, London EC1V 9LB

Copyright © Richard Wurmbrand 1982

First published by Marshall Morgan & Scott 1982

All rights reserved. No part of this publication may be
reproduced, stored in a retrieval system, or transmitted, in
any form or by any means, electronic, mechanical, photo-
copying, recording or otherwise, without the prior
permission of the Copyright owner.

ISBN 0 551 00937 3

Text set by
Rowland Phototypesetting Ltd
Bury St Edmunds, Suffolk
Printed in Great Britain by
Richard Clay Ltd, Bungay

Contents

To the precious souls known
only by God, who support
the persecuted in prayer.

Introduction

A man driving through the streets of Los Angeles with his five-year-old son was about to pass one of its many churches when the child suddenly exclaimed, 'Daddy, stop! Let's go in the church and find out how God is doing today.'

An excellent question. How does God fare?

How would you fare if your dearest children were being tortured?

In recent years, tens of thousands of Christians and Buddhists have passed through the so-called re-education camps in Vietnam. Many are still there. In one of these camps the specialist in beatings is Tu Cao. He boasts of having whipped 2000 prisoners, 500 of whom died.

Some fifty prisoners are assembled in the prison yard. One of them, Tran Tien Tai, has been sentenced to thirty lashes. Brought naked from his cell, he must stretch out on the earth, with his face to the ground.

Tu Cao plays with his whip. He touches the hips of his victim to appreciate the resistance of the flesh and measure his strokes accordingly. He is not allowed to kill.

The prisoners are ordered to look straight at what is happening. It is forbidden to avert one's face.

After the fifth stroke, Tai, unable to bear it any longer, shouts, '*Troi oi. Chua oi.* (Woe, woe, my God.)'

The beating is interrupted. The prison director says, 'It is not permitted to shout during physical punishment. The first five strokes do not count. Begin again.'

The counting starts over. *One, two, three, . . . twenty, . . . twenty-five . . .* Tai does not cry out any more. It appears that he has passed away.

. . . Thirty. 'Up!' orders the officer. The prisoner does not move. 'You refuse to obey?' No reaction. The officer bends over the corpse and says triumphantly, 'He has committed suicide. He has bitten off his tongue and swallowed it. It is his fault. The revolution does not kill

men, neither does it torture. If it punishes, it does so like a father punishing his child.' (*The Vietnamese Gulag*, by Doan van Toai, Laffont Publ. House, France)

Christ is tortured still.

In Communist Romania, if a prisoner did not betray the secrets of the underground Church to the interrogator, the warden was told, 'Take him to Major Brinzaru or to Comrade Vidal.' Brinzaru was the most skilled torturer. Vidal was a female officer who specialized in beating male prisoners on the testicles.

In the U.S.S.R., the order would be, 'Take him to Dr. Temo or to Mladionov.'

Dr. Temo would always receive the prisoner with a smile. He wore a physician's white coat and was uniformly polite. He would call bishops 'Eminence' and persons of high rank 'Excellency' and would explain in soft speech, 'My role is only to prepare the psychological conditions for openness in your discussions with the interrogator.' For this purpose, he drove needles under fingernails. A doctor accustomed to sterile technique, he would never practise his craft without first disinfecting the needle.

As for Mladionov, his special assignment was to sodomize nuns or Christian girls. Once, when a Baptist girl was given into his hands, she spoke to him with such sweetness and love that he left her unharmed and was converted. In retaliation, the Communists went to his home, hanged him, and left hurriedly. Brethren who entered the house immediately after their departure cut down the body, discovered that the knot had not been well made, and brought Mladionov back to life. After that, he had to live in hiding. (*Irina*, by H. Hartfeld, Christian Herald Press, USA)

There are zones of memory where every touch draws blood. For this reason, prisoners try to forget their children. Remembering them is too painful. But the Communists, aware of their vulnerability, force them to tread the mine-fields of the mind. In long nights of interrogation, the names of the children would be brought up continually.

Tapes containing the screams and weeping of children were played outside the cell doors. Every prisoner was sure he recognized the voices of his own offspring.

In the Secret Police in Odessa was a young Communist girl, Vera Grebenniukova, who cut off ears and bits of the privy parts of prisoners.

In some areas children have been beaten to make them betray their friends. One group of 11- to 15-year-olds were beaten and then driven by car through the streets so that, in case they could not remember the names of fellow 'law-breakers,' they could at least point out the children who should be arrested.

One form of torment the Communists enjoy is to put sane persons in cells with raving madmen. In Savastopol, 18 prisoners were crammed into a room without windows, three steps long by one and a half wide. Since they could not all find room to stand, some hung leaning on the shoulders of others. They suffocated for lack of air.

Others have been undressed in winter, put in a pit, and doused with water. Still other prisoners had their skulls encircled with a thin rope, which was attached to a stick that was turned to tighten the rope until the scalp separated from the skull.

The torturer who perpetrated these cruelties was a former clown who had given up making children laugh in order to make men scream. (*The Red Terror in Russia*, by S. Melgunov. Brandy, N. Y., 1979)

These things happened under Lenin. His successor refined his techniques and extended his scope. Stalin killed the Christians Odintsev and Peter Vins, who shine among the millions of others. The killings have continued under Khrushchev and Brezhnev: the Baptists Khmara, Moiseev, Ostapenko, Biblenko, Deynega, Lambdin. Who but the angels in heaven can chronicle the names of all those members of the body of Christ in whom He is tortured still?

In Nicaragua, where guerrillas gained the victory, four priests came to power in the government along with the

Communists. One of the latter, a Mrs. Astorga, renowned for her beauty, gained notoriety when she lured into her house General Vega of the former regime. Here guerrillas were ready and waiting. She watched while the General was beaten, his eyes gouged out, and his private parts cut off and stuffed in his mouth. What a comrade-in-arms for priests and pastors! (*The Rock*, May 1981)

The Adventist Nina Rujetshko was tortured to death in the prison of Kemerovsk on January 1, 1980. In the Solikamsk camp the Adventist Simeon Baholdin was killed on November 11, 1980. ('Communication from the Soviet Adventist Leadership')

Prisoners were executed in a Siberian camp because, desperately hungry, they had killed and eaten a guard dog. (*Coming Out of the Ice*, by V. Hermann)

The Ukrainian Catholic priests Gorgula and Kotyk were also killed. The Communists bound one, poured gasoline over him, and set him afire. The second was found covered with blood, with all his teeth broken and his mouth stuffed with bread, in mockery of Holy Communion. (*Catacombes*, France, May 1981)

The Communists have killed wantonly for decades. *Russkaia Misl*, France, of July 16, reminded readers that Kalmikov, leader of the Communist Kabardino-Balkar Republic (U.S.S.R.), easily disposed of all opposition: He invited the Moslem clergy and heads of tribes for peaceful talks and then killed them all.

The Soviet secret printing press 'True Witness,' which publishes mainly religious but also political anti-Communist material, has printed a book of verse entitled *Oxana* that describes the suffering of the Lithuanian Christian Poshkene Birute. She was deprived of her children and put into a psychiatric asylum because of her faith in Christ.

The Communist newspaper *Niamunas* slandered her by claiming she tried to poison her children, though she was not charged with this crime. It also alleged that believers appear naked in their meetings and engage in sexual orgies.

The pastor's wife is said to be his fourth.

In her poem, our sister evokes the martyrs of the past and concludes: 'The murdered are silent; we continue. There is no more beautiful fate than to fight and suffer, to be men persecuted for the truth. Prisons, camps, asylums, shootings—how powerless are these false ideas of hatred. The snow melts in the spring. It cannot destroy the sun's rays. Neither can wickedness destroy love. It will be conquered.'

In spite of the terror, Soviet Lithuania is flooded with religious publications secretly printed: *The Chronicle of the Catholic Church*, *The Dawn*, *The Future*, *God and Country*, *Blood*, and *The Suffering Christ*, among others.

The faith, hope, and reason of Soviet Christians have not been banished. These dedicated believers will not give up their eternal reward out of fear of suffering. For them the fire of persecution is cool and violence is impotent.

The Communists may cut out the tongue of the Baptist Khmara, who sang songs of praise to God, but the song remains.

Families of Christian prisoners have difficulty obtaining food. But what about the prisoners themselves?

In the Kolyma camp, prisoners were so famished that they ate the corpse of a horse that had been lying dead for more than a week. It stank and was covered with maggots. At the Autini goldfields, prisoners ate the lubricating grease intended to oil the wheelbarrows. (Solzhenitsyn, *Gulag Archipelago*). I ate worse than that when I was in Romanian Communist jails.

In the Solovetsk camps (U.S.S.R.) the corpses of those who froze during the laboring day were left on the site. One had frozen with his head bent down between his knees— Elijah's position in prayer (I Kings 18:42). Two were frozen back to back against each other. (D. Vitkovski, *Half a Lifetime*). Cold water had been poured on naked prisoners in winter.

In Czechoslovakia, Communists killed a leading personality of the underground Church, the secretly ordained priest Premysl Coufal. He had been taken many times to the police and told he had the choice of informing on the believers or accepting death. The last time he was called in, they gave him a calendar with February 23 circled. This was the deadline for a reply. Day after day Coufal looked at the calendar. Should he become a Judas or a martyr? He was a child of God. He remained faithful and paid the ultimate price.

The Communists entered his apartment, smashed his skull, broke his nose, and made cuts in his arms, then turned on the gas. Later, they allowed Christians to see what they had done. They wanted to scare others who follow Jesus and testify that Communism is wicked. (*Bayerkurier*, Germany, April 18, 1981)

Would you openly oppose the evil in your community if you knew that suffering awaited you?

The Dutch couple Barendsen, evangelical missionaries in Communist Afghanistan, testified for Jesus in this country that has been subdued by Soviet hate. They were bound to chairs and cut to pieces. Before returning to Afghanistan after a furlough, they had been asked if they did not fear to go back. They replied, 'We know only one great danger: not to be in the center of God's will.'

The Lebanese evangelical Jameel Safoury taught the blind about the wickedness of men and about the Light of the world. For this, leftist Palestinian guerrillas cut off his arms and his head. The corpse was found under a bridge. (*Idea*, Germany, April 13)

The Romanian George Bratianu was driven to suicide. The Communists secured his hands behind his back, then tied living rats around his neck, which nibbled away at his skin and flesh. He jumped through a window to his death. (*Tara Si Exiulul*, Spain, February 1981)

Brethren in Russian prisons endure monstrous torture. Some are put on their bellies, their hands are tied to their feet, and then they are lifted by ropes to the ceiling, then raised and lowered repeatedly until they faint. At this point, they are revived with a bucket of water and the torture starts all over again. From time to time a doctor examines them and says, 'You can continue.' (Krasnov-Levitin, *Toward the New City*). They remain faithful.

A courier of the Christian Mission to the Communist World met a Chinese, now 82 years old. He travels everywhere on an old bicycle. The courier was able to give him a new Bible, for which he was most grateful, even though he had to cycle 200 miles to receive it.

He asked this mission if he could be given a new bike because the old one was worn out. He had ridden thousands of miles in two years taking the Word of God to people who yearned after it.

Solzhenitsyn, in recounting his experiences in the Gulag, tells how at a certain moment he realized he had abandoned hope of liberation. At that time he was receiving a starvation ration and yet was expected to work twelve hours a day at hard labor. In addition, he had a malignant tumor, and physicians were already predicting his death.

One day, while shoveling sand under a scorching sun, he simply stopped working, though he knew the guards would beat him, perhaps to death. He simply could not go on.

Suddenly, he was aware that someone was standing near him. Turning, he saw an old man, who with his cane made the sign of the cross in the sand. From that redemptive gesture, Solzhenitsyn understood that we do not have to fear death. He who was crucified was also resurrected.

We too have that hope. Christians have no reason to despair. Neither do they need hypocrisy. They can afford to live lives that are transparent before God, even though they, their churches, and their institutions might perish because of their integrity. They know that beyond the cross is the resurrection.

The Soviet Christians Petker, Friesen and Peters were killed in an automobile accident while transporting Bibles that had been secretly printed. As in many other cases, the accident was probably staged by the Communists. When Sister Petker wept, her three-year-old child asked,

'Mommy, where is Daddy?' She replied, 'With the Saviour.' Inspired by an angel, the child then said, 'If so, why do you weep?'

Those who have suffered greatly are surrounded by angels and a cloud of witnesses. They preach as others cannot. Obviously, a person who has cheerfully borne a heavy cross speaks with a voice different from that of one whose knowledge is only from books.

It is said about the imprisoned Romanian Orthodox priest Calciu that he is in agony, that he has lost half his weight and is almost deaf and blind. He has already been in jail sixteen years. One can sense this fact when reading the sermons that led to his new arrest.

In spite of all his suffering he writes: 'Without resurrection, man would be the most unhappy being on earth, because plants and animals don't know they will die, whereas we are haunted by the idea. I will die, perhaps even today, though I am young.

'Atheists forbid any belief in the resurrection. But without it, what is the sense of the short interval between birth and death? Atheists themselves fear their own disappearance at death. Mausoleums have been erected to their leaders, a tragic substitute for the soul's innate aspiration for eternity.

'Jesus has offered us a death without fear, an understanding between death and happiness, because He provided the guarantee that death is not an end, but the beginning of eternal life.'

Calciu does not fear death. He sees an angel in the midst of the whirlwind.

The abbot of a secret Catholic convent in the Ukraine wrote as follows to Cardinal Slipyi, who himself had been in Soviet jails for 17 years: 'Day and night we are in adoration before the Holy Sacrament. A few young girls have taken perpetual vows. In hospitals, secret nuns are a magnificent witness to nurses. Thus many seekers find the way to Christ.'

The Russian Orthodox Christian prisoner Poresh recalls that in court, from his defendant's position, he could see the cross on a church steeple and that, as he received his sentence, it seemed bathed in a strange light. He wrote from jail: 'Many ask themselves how to receive the Spirit. Sacrifice yourself in His service. Give blood, and receive the Spirit.'

*   *   *

How does God fare today? Well, he suffers greatly. Our Creator, our Father in heaven suffers.

You ask what happens to Christ today? Well, He is tortured still. What Christians endure becomes His pain. They are His body.

God has given me the assignment to be a voice for those martyred for their faith in Christ.

*   *   *

Who is Richard Wurmbrand? you may ask.

Since no one can speak objectively or without bias about himself, I have chosen to let others testify about me first, both pro and con. You, the reader, may judge for yourself.

Fifteen years have passed since I founded the mission 'Jesus to the Communist World', after having spent fourteen years in Communist prisons.

This anniversary might be important for me – what is its importance to others? Should a book be written for this occasion? What happened during this period that could be of interest to you?

Let us see what friends and foes alike have to say about me:

No contemporary person has meant so much for the opening of the eyes of the West to what is going on in the Communist camp – except the much decried Wurmbrand. Before Wurmbrand came, we spoke to deaf ears.

The Rev Michael Bourdeaux, Director of
the Institute for Study of Religion and
Communism, London

Wurmbrand irritates, but opens our eyes . . . Wurmbrand has got the world to hearken, even if he has sacrificed himself. He has reached quite a bit . . . Wurmbrand has shouted the cry of the martyrs.

> The Rev Ingemar Martinson, General Secretary of
> the Slavic Mission, Sweden

Wurmbrand is an Iron Curtain Paul. He is the most authoritative voice of the Underground Church, more than a living martyr.

> *Underground Evangelism*

Since the Sermon on the Mount was delivered, no one has preached with love like Richard Wurmbrand.

> *Haratta*, Finland

Wurmbrand has brought to the universal Church a new dimension, reminding it about the martyrs.

> *Church Times*, London

Wurmbrand burst like a fireball across the cool complacency of some.

> USA Congressional Record

We were hit by a hurricane called Wurmbrand.

> *Tablet*, New Zealand

We have checked and can say with almost certainty that there has never been a Pastor Wurmbrand in Romania.

> Finnish Communist newspaper

The manifestations of Wurmbrand are determined by high emotions, they are without compromise and often naive . . . His judgments about church politics prove a terrifying narrowness . . . The danger of Wurmbrand's grotesque distortions consists in the fact that he calls Christian groups in Eastern Europe to resistance until death . . .

> Gerhard Simon in *The Churches in Russia*

In the present Communist regimes strong powers for the humanisation of society lie hidden . . . Wurmbrand becomes really dangerous.

> Van de Heuwel, then Director of Public Relations,
> The World Council of Churches

Pastor Richard Wurmbrand possesses a bordello and nine night clubs in the USA.

From the Soviet film *The Emissaries*, which has as its target the smuggling of religious literature into USSR, organised by 'Jesus to the Communist World'.

Wurmbrand is the devil's mouthpiece.

Arbeiterzeitung, Switzerland

Wurmbrand is a new St John the Baptist . . . a voice crying in the wilderness.

Christianity Today, USA

Wurmbrand is a Marxist theologian.

The Pilgrim, USA

Wurmbrand is a passionate anti-Communist and anti-Soviet. His books are full of unveiled hatred.

Several Soviet newspapers

Wurmbrand completely rejects scholarly objectivity.

Reformatorisch Dagbladett, Holland

Wurmbrand is a red pastor.

Vaderland, South Africa

Wurmbrand misuses the pulpit for spreading his political views.

The Swedish Lutheran Bishop Strom in *Dalademokraten*

Wurmbrand is one of the most active voices of anti-Communism.

Polititcheskoie Samoabrazovanie, Moscow

Except the Bible, nothing has shaken me like Wurmbrand's *Tortured for Christ*. It is the message of the century. Even more: since the persecution of Christians by Nero, it is the most powerful Acts of Martyrs.

Dr Kurt Koch, renowned German evangelical pastor and author

Wurmbrand is broadly charitable in his understanding of God's love and the nature of man. Not even an ounce of contentiousness appears in his books. Perhaps the agony of long imprisonment purges that out of a man.

Alliance Witness, USA

Wurmbrand suffered beastly treatment by the Communists, so he has remained with a confused mind. He is not

Evangelical, so he cannot be trusted. He is rather a mystic.

A Dutch Christian magazine

Wurmbrand is intemperate.

Catholic Herald, London

Wurmbrand speaks softly, without flourished comparisons and without dramatic exaggerations . . . His concepts of Christianity come from the original sources . . . Loud promotion does not correspond to his character. Richard Wurmbrand is surprisingly near to the Nazarene whom he represents. Weak in health, he catches through unyielding spiritual power. He descends from the podium exhausted and has made his audience ashamed rather than inflamed.

Berner Tagblatt, Switzerland

Wurmbrand is a dirty Jew.

Christian Vanguard, USA

Wurmbrand has been pro-Nazi.

Verden Gang, Norway

Wurmbrand, a fascinating and passionate (sometimes even excessively so) personality, appears always firm in the fight against the skepticism of occidental Christianity, which, with rare exceptions, cannot believe that Communism might be a menace for her.

La Suisse, Switzerland

Wurmbrand's book 'If that were Christ would you give Him your blanket' convinces one to give his blanket not only to one's persecuted brother, but even to one's persecutor, so full of love is it.

Nuova Republica, Italy

The denunciations of tortures and barbarisms in the Communist camp made by Wurmbrand are more moving than those of Solzhenitsyn.

Il Citadino, Italy

Wurmbrand's attacks on Communist treatment of Christian prisoners was viewed by many as sensationalistic until Solzhenitsyn's *Gulag Archipelago* confirmed his descriptions of the atrocities.

Daily News, California

Thank God for men like Solzhenitsyn and Wurmbrand. Both have written books of their imprisonment in Communist countries. These books have been made available to us for a reason – a divine warning.

Tacoma News Tribune, USA

Some church leaders in the West attack Pastor Richard Wurmbrand, the leading fighter for the Underground Church, accusing him of lying and exaggerating regarding the atrocities in Communist prisons. I have personally met Christians who sat in prison with Wurmbrand. They told me, 'Not only is everything which Wurmbrand says true, but much, much more. Nobody can describe the ferocious things happening there.'

Mrs Anutza Moise, author of
'A ransom for Wurmbrand' in
Morgenbladet, Norway

Rev Richard Wurmbrand still bears the marks on his body of hideous Communist tortures. He is an internationally respected author, lecturer and evangelist.

Boston Herald, USA

The publicity given Solzhenitsyn has brought to light the truth of Wurmbrand's outspoken statements. Should we not back up Wurmbrand and his Christ-like mission to the Communist world?

Reformatio, Switzerland

Both Solzhenitsyn and Wurmbrand are giants in modern church history.

Dagen, Norway

Pastor Wurmbrand is wrong in practising an undeserved generosity with the enemies of the human race. The love sorrily shown by him surpasses even that shown by God, who, instead of sharing his bread with Lucifer, chased him from heaven with a fiery sword. He was not gentler with Adam and Eve when they trespassed, but showed them the door by which they should leave paradise. Jesus, when he met the merchants, took a whip.

Vatra, Romanian emigration magazine

President Carter attacks Russia for her denials of human rights, but makes no mention of similar denials in China. Why? The answer is plain. China has no voice like that of Richard Wurmbrand to plead her cause.

Life of Faith, Britain

A Jew like St Paul, a convert like him, Wurmbrand jumps from one continent to another, bringing his message everywhere: Help the Christians in the catacombs. For us, the action of Pastor Wurmbrand is an affirmation not only of Christianity, but also of the Romanian nation.

Cuvantul Romanesc, Romanian emigration newspaper

Wurmbrand through his total self-sacrifice has opened eyes in the West, as a result of which an innumerable multitude takes part in the fate of our persecuted brethren in faith of all denominations.

Neue Bildpost, West Germany

Pastor R. Wurmbrand could be envied by the most aggressive professional football player. His voice is savage. He will have a tragic end. He was in prison because he illegally printed and spread religious propaganda, inciting believers to oppose authorities. He is a demonised pastor.

Nauka i Religia, Central Atheist Magazine, Moscow

Since my coming to the West sixteen years ago, myths have arisen that portray me alternatively as a modern day saint or as a villain. Some who spoke badly about me in the beginning later became my friends. Some who spoke well of me have changed their mind since. What triggered this controversy around my person? I believe it was the fact that God used me for founding the world-wide fellowship Christian Missions to the Communist World.

What sort of mission is this?

While writing this book I often have before my eyes the scene of my arrest in 1959 and my wife, Sabina, running after the van of the Secret Police. And I also have the impression that Christians from Communist countries are running behind me crying, 'Speak out, speak out for us'.

Their cries made me found the mission Jesus to the Communist World, and prompted me to write its story.

I do not believe in histories. The word 'history' never

occurs in the Bible. The reality of all times is one whole entity unfolding. It is like a motion picture. We see thousands of things happening on the screen, any one action seeming to be the result of preceding causes. While the film is on its reel, and the reel not yet in motion, all these events exist and occur at the same time. Only when the film is running do they appear to succeed one another. Likewise, the absence of a mission like ours, its appearance, its joys, its successes and failures have existed all along on the reel of God's master plan. We humans discover what has been foreordained by God only by instalments, day by day.

As a Christian wishing to be honest, I will add one more thing about history: no history can be written except from a particular point of view. Even the biblical narratives are subject to this principle. Their stories are not expressions of facts alone, but also ideological convictions, for there is no such thing as objective truth in historical matters.

For example, the author of the book of Chronicles was probably a Levite, for in his book the Levites are mentioned a hundred times as against once in the books of Kings and twice in the books of Samuel, although they all report the same events. Furthermore, we can easily guess to which tribe the author was related by marriage because the tribe of Judah is mentioned in 102 verses in the book of Chronicles, the tribe of Levi in 81, and the remaining ten tribes in only 186 altogether.

No one can, or should, write objective history. There are seventeen passages in the Bible telling about the twelve sons of Jacob – each passage enumerating the names in a different order, according to the writer's preference. One who has no preference is not human and should not write. Even Jesus had a preferred disciple, and God a preferred nation. The preferences shown in biblical history prove it is inspired by God.

I am writing this book not as a scholarly history but as a song of love toward the Underground Church and, as in the Bible narratives, there will be many other elements in my song beside historical facts.

1: The Beginning

There is no Zero in the Bible

It all began in a prison cell in Communist Romania in 1948.

I was in solitary confinement, thirty feet beneath the earth. I had lost my church, my family, my liberty, my health. Even my name. My captors had forbidden me ever to pronounce it, so that guards would not be able to disclose where I was. The Communists had done everything to reduce me to nothing, a zero, but they did not succeed.

The Gospels tell how the Lord Jesus multiplied seven loaves and fed thousands of people with them.

Suppose the disciples had not had seven loaves but only three or one. What would have happened? The multitudes would have been satisfied all the same. As a matter of fact, on another occasion Jesus had only five loaves of bread instead of seven. Nonetheless, he fed an even bigger multitude with an even greater number of baskets of leftovers (Mark 8:19-21). You can serve God with very little. His blessings do not depend upon the size or quantity of your gift, but on the spirit in which you bring it to him.

Suppose I have no bread – zero bread – to bring; what then? This is impossible. The languages in which the Bible was written, Hebrew, Aramaic and Greek, have neither the word 'zero' nor its mathematical symbol 'o'. The Bible knows of no one who has nothing to bring to Jesus. You can bring your own person, the very person who claims, 'I possess nothing', for you do have something very valuable: yourself and your utter poverty.

Who are the Underground Christians?

A man who was technically a zero in a prison cell thought about helping the persecuted church: this is how our mission was conceived. I was in prison with many Romanian underground Christians. I met Soviet underground Christians when their army occupied my homeland. Later I met others from many different Communist countries. What kind of men are they? A few incidents from their lives will help you understand them better than theoretical explanations.

A believer released from a Lithuanian prison, where he had served a sentence for his faith, wrote: 'My outward appearance is not attractive. In the slave labour camp I worked beneath the earth, and had an accident which broke my back. Later I went to visit a Christian family. One of the children stared at me and asked, "Uncle, what do you have on your back?" Sure that some mockery would follow, I answered, "A hunchback." "No," said the child, "God is Love and gives no one deformities. You do not have a hunchback, but a box below your shoulders. In this box are angelic wings. Some day the box will open and you will fly to heaven with these wings." I began to cry for joy. Even now, as I write, I am crying.'

Such children and former prisoners are characteristic of the underground Christians in Communist countries.

We received a letter from Romania telling us that a Communist, a former head of the Secret Police, now director of a great state enterprise, had heard one of our broadcasts and was inspired to change his ways and give his heart to the Lord. The following Sunday he went to the Baptist church, prayed publicly and asked forgiveness for all his wickedness. The whole congregation, well aware of his past, wept with him. He was immediately expelled from the Communist Party and dismissed from his office. Although he now earns his bread as a simple worker, he has the joy that passes all understanding because he belongs to the Lord.

Many members of the martyred church have given up privileged positions in order to serve Christ.

Nauka i Religia, a Russian atheistic magazine, described Russia's heroic Christian children. The reporter said, 'After a religious service in Kislovodsk, I spoke with a girl of eleven. She is sincerely convinced that while she prays, the good Lord looks at her and smiles. She says, "God exists. I see him myself. I do not believe anyone who says that he does not exist." Another little girl kissed an image showing Jesus crucified. Then she made her doll kiss it too. When asked why, she said, "Jesus looked at the doll. I saw it."'

I am convinced, too, that God is very much interested in the dolls with which little girls are playing. I am also convinced that the children, and the adults, who lead such a heavy fight against atheism must be helped.

Zaria Vostoka describes the trial of a group of believers in Suhum, in the Soviet Union. Their crime consisted in gathering twenty children in a wood to teach them the Christian faith. The atheist Topuria was surprised to find out that his son was among the young believers. The child, called as witness in court, was encouraged loudly by his father to speak out against the defendants. The boy, Nodar, answered: 'You are my temporary, earthly father. My heavenly, eternal Father is our God, Jehovah.' The accused were sentenced to two to five years in prison and were deprived forever of their children.

Solzhenitsyn, the Russian Nobel prize winner expelled from his country, tells in the third volume of *Gulag Archipelago* the story of an evangelist. This man had published no volumes of sermons, was never on TV, had no mass rallies. Not even his name was certain. Solzhenitsyn says only that, 'it seems to have been Alexander Sisoiev.'

Just as the creed says no word about the sermons of Jesus, but only that he 'suffered under Pontius Pilate, was crucified and buried,' history only tells us about the man 'perhaps called Sisoiev' that he was an evangelist and that he was shot in the Kengir concentration camp having spent many years in prison enjoying quiet communion with his Lord.

At that time, shooting of the innocent was an everyday occurrence. But this man, 'perhaps called Sisoiev', had been a man apart. Those who saw him 'took knowledge that he had been with Jesus', though he was unlearned and ignorant like Peter and John (Acts 4:13). The camp inmates had been resigned to the beating and shooting of other prisoners, but when this saint whose name is not even known was shot, the whole camp of 2,500 common prisoners – among whom were murderers, burglars, thieves, and 500 political prisoners – rebelled. They refused to work and attacked the guards. Their main request was that the person responsible for the shooting of the evangelist be punished.

In the end, the Communists quenched the revolt having killed about seven hundred political prisoners and criminals, who died showing their love for and solidarity with a man about whom we know nothing except that he knew how to keep his privacy and to commune in quietness with God, that he possessed an inner closet even in a common prison cell.

Perhaps instead of having conferences about modern methods of evangelism it is more important for us to be like the one 'whose name was perhaps Sisoiev'.

Castro attended the execution of a Christian by a firing squad. As his hands were tied behind his back, Castro told him, 'Kneel and beg for your life.' The Christian shouted back, 'I kneel for no man.' A sharp-shooter put a bullet through first one knee, then the other. Castro exulted, 'You see, we made you kneel.' The man was then slowly killed, shot by shot through the non-vital parts of the body, prolonging his agony.

The devil himself works through these anti-Christian dictators. We hear again the words he said to our Lord, 'All these things will I give thee, if thou wilt fall down and worship me' (Matt. 4:9).

'God is dead and religion is a lie,' is the slogan spread daily in Albania, which declared itself 'The first atheist state of the world'. Of two hundred priests, only fourteen are still alive, twelve of them in concentration camps. Two thousand mosques and churches have been destroyed. The cathedral of Tirana became a sports hall, mosques were changed into public toilets. The results of this atheist terror? A group of 116 young couples were discovered to have gathered in Fier for a collective marriage ceremony. The Albanian Communist press declares that Christians tattoo a cross on their palm, Moslems a crescent, to make it clear from the first handshake that they stick to their faith in God.

B. had been a Communist state prosecutor in Romania. He fell foul of the Party and was imprisoned by his own comrades. Being in the same cell with Pastor Richard Wurmbrand, he told how he had been transferred from a prison where hunger reigned to a mine where the prisoners were given more food since they had to do hard slave labour. At the prison gate he was met by a stranger who immediately offered him some food and sat down near him while he ate. The former prosecutor asked the stranger for how long he was sentenced. The reply was twenty years.

'What for?'

'For giving some food to a fugitive pastor sought by the police.'

'Who gave you such punishment for a good deed?'

'You were the state prosecutor at my trial. You did not recognise me, but I recognised you. I am a Christian. Christ taught us to reward evil with good. I wished to teach you that it is right to give food to a hungry man.'

Dr Munteanu's father, an Orthodox dean, had been killed for being a priest. The doctor eventually ended up in prison with the murderers of his father. When the murderers fell sick, he gave them not only medical care but also his own bread and food.

The Christian Tsotsea had been sentenced unjustly to twenty years in prison. After a while, the judge who sentenced him was also imprisoned and fell deathly ill. His sickness was repulsive. His waste and urine had to be washed away continually under prison conditions, without running water, cotton or sheets. Tsotsea, the victim, loved his enemy and cared for him as for a brother until the judge died, reconciled with God and forgiven.

A vision in a solitary prison cell

Let me proceed in my story.

When I was in prison I had not heard about the discoveries of antique scrolls in Qumran written by a sect which divided the world into two camps: the sons of light, and the sons of darkness, with nothing in-between. Yet, from studying the Bible, I had learned to think in the same terms.

Since I have been in the West, I have often been reproached for painting everything solely in black and white: Christians are white, atheists black; the Red block is evil, the free world good. I accept this reproach. Jesus never used the word 'grey'; it does not occur a single time in the New Testament.

As it was, the sons of darkness, the Communists, had taken over our country through terror and deceit. Thousands of sons and daughters of light sat in jail. I was one of them, kept in solitary confinement. There was nothing to disturb me in my cell. We had neither the Bible nor any other book, not even a scrap of paper to distract us. For years we could do nothing but gaze at mouldy walls.

My whole past as a preacher seemed to me to have been superficial. I felt that the Word of God is best spoken through closed lips. Jesus had been almost mute on the question of God until the age of thirty. And even then he spoke little. Why should he speak? Does a flower ever shout? For Jesus the simple fact of being spoke eloquently enough.

I am Jewish, as was Jesus. Unlike the Greeks, Assyrians, and the Egyptians, ancient Israel left no paintings, sculpture, or monuments to admire. Jews could not see why men need to create works of art when there are so many mountains and brooks, tulips and children to be admired. They did not understand life as we understand it with our modern science. Nor did they sense life as artists do. They trans-understood reality: they looked through reality to God and found him to be undepictable. All that remains from the ancient Jews is some poetry expressing their awe before God. Had God not bid them write this down, they would not have done it. When you enter into relationship with God, the best communication is silence. 'The Lord is in his holy temple; let all the earth keep silence before him' (Hab. 2:20).

So I did not suffer from the lack of paper and ink. Where could I have found words to write what was in my heart? Silence that continues long enough acquires its own sound.

I heard the Word which cannot be written because it is neither substantive, nor verb, nor adjective. It had become flesh.

I had reached another state. By a mere act of will I could evoke persons, perfumes, garlands, food, drink, song, music, angels, men, women. Whatever I set my heart on would rise up before me. The easiest to realise was the presence of Jesus. The etymology of the Sanskrit word *hrdayam*, from which the English 'heart' derives, is *hrdy ayam*, which means 'God is in the heart'. There is no Sanskrit word for 'heart' apart from 'God'. A heart without him is not worthy of this name.

I fantasised much. I imagined what I would do if I were the Pope, the President of the United States, a merchant, a world-traveller, a poet, a beggar. I dreamt how I would lead my life if I were young again.

The Bible tells about a miracle that occurred in the time of the Jewish king Hezekiah: the shadow on the sun-dial receded ten degrees. Let us presume this event took place at 8 p.m., setting the time back to 10 a.m. and so enabling the king to re-make the decisions of that day. He could undo all his mistakes and sins. Thus could I do, too, I fancied, if I could be a boy and start my life again.

Dreamers play a special role in God's plan.

Moses wrote about a pharaoh who had been every inch a king. Not only did he act as a king when awake; his subconscious, too, was concerned with the welfare of his people and he would dream about it at night. This dreamer of good met another 'dreamer of dreams' (Gen. 37:19), who was at the other extreme of the social spectrum: a prisoner from a foreign nation, an innocent sentenced unjustly for attempted rape. His name was Joseph. These two dreamers united, and as a result, Egypt was spared from famine and could even feed starving people from neighbouring countries.

I dreamt also during that solitary time, and I greatly valued dreams. Sometimes they were nightmares; at other times they were just a pleasant pastime. But there were some dreams of great significance.

My most beloved dream was to be an ideal bride for Christ and to caress him rather than serve him.

I had time to ponder over many subjects. The years of solitude were long.

One of my frequent dreams was that one day I would be free in the West, that I would be able to describe the rule of the sons of darkness to the world, and that I would organise practical help for its victims.

This dream arose in me as a kind of foreknowledge. In 1 Kings, where we are told about the construction of the temple of Jerusalem under King Solomon, the Hebrew word *behibanotoh* is used, which is an exceptional form of the verb 'to construct'. Literally translated, it means that the building built itself. Thus the temple was not constructed by men, but arose of its own accord. Men only gave it a material shape.

Likewise, a servant to whom a pound had been entrusted told the lord who had given it to him, 'Thy pound has gained ten pounds' (Luke 19:16), not, 'I earned another ten pounds through my skill.' Such things often happen by themselves.

In the same way, I did not see myself and others creating an organisation in my dreams. Rather, I foresaw an organisation building itself. I foresaw my future activities. I did not have to decide them, which does not mean, however, that I did not have to think about them.

Thinking in jail about secret missionary work

Obviously I did not spend the whole time dreaming. I also thought, in the real sense of this word.

There was one thing I knew for sure I would not do: I would not agitate against the Communists. I loved them.

Philo of Alexandria describes Pilate as guilty of acts of corruption, insults, rapine, intrigues, arrogance, repeated murders of innocent victims and constant savagery. The ancient historian Josephus Flavius gives the same description of him. The Talmud has very negative words about the high priests in Jesus' time. But the Gospels use no such epithets. This is because the evangelists did not hate. They said only what was needed to stimulate faith and action, not what would make their adversary despicable in the eyes of others.

Love is the only possible attitude of a Christian. The tree does not withdraw its protecting shadow from the woodcutter, nor the moon its light from the hovel of the outcast.

Instead of agitating against Communism, I would smuggle the Word of God into Communist countries.

I had no scruples about becoming a smuggler. It is written in Exodus 35:3, 'Ye shall kindle no fire throughout your habitations upon the Sabbath day.' But in Leviticus 6:5, priests are further commanded to see that the fire upon the altar shall be kept burning perpetually: 'The priest shall kindle wood on it every morning,' which includes the Sabbath. Just as these two commands are exceptions to each other, the smuggling of Bibles is an exception to the basic principle not to mislead men.

Prolonged systematic thinking was not possible in a state of extreme hunger. I was only able to think sporadically, while I tried to keep my mind healthy, knowing that a mind is too precious to waste. It is only now that I can systematise the thoughts which occurred to me then.

Will we not have to deceive? Will we not have to break laws for this? What is wrong with breaking laws in order to give eternal life to those who break the bodies of Christians, only because these persecutors do not know the truth? The battle against Communism is a battle fought by the will of the Lord. In such a battle no sin touches you, because you are acting as a messenger of the Lord.

To build an altar and to offer sacrifices outside the Temple Mount in Jerusalem was an action contrary to the law of God. Yet the prophet Elijah did it (1 Kgs. 18:32). Exceptional measures are permitted to meet exceptional circumstances. This was to be our case also.

I knew the Communists would try to hinder our activity. They had infiltrated the Church in Romania and other Communist countries already. If we were to create such an organisation abroad, they would be sure to spy on it.

I remembered the Dreyfus case, the Jewish officer in the French army who was sentenced for treason only because he had been a Jew. After he had spent ten years on Devil's Island, a minute fragment of a letter written by the German military attaché was discovered in the wastepaper of the German embassy which was routinely delivered to the

French counter-espionage section. This piece of writing proved that it was not Dreyfus but a Major Eszterhazi who had had treasonable connections. Dreyfus was rehabilitated. In his case French justice had been misled. The Communists would try to create confusion in our ranks too.

So the organisation which I envisioned would have to be very careful even in the West. I did not know at that time that shredding machines existed. Now we have one in the office of the Christian Mission to the Communist World. No bit of paper is thrown away. And we keep absolutely no archives. They are kept on microfilm in a private home. In an emergency everything can be burnt in a minute. I did not foresee that some solutions could be so simple, but I knew that security measures would have to be taken.

The silence I learned in my isolated cell was to be useful. I became interested in the silences of the Gospel, in the stories which were left out as well as those which were put in. The Gospel tells the story of the conversion of an unpleasant person, the persecutor Saul of Tarsus. From my point of view it would have been far more interesting to know how James, the brother of the Lord, who opposed him during his earthly life was later converted and took the place of another James, the brother of Zebedee, in the inner circle of the apostles. I would also have liked to know stories of the heroes of faith persecuted by Saul. The biblical authors must have had good motives for remaining silent about these matters: they might have involved persons who needed to be protected. So we would have to be cautious too, and know when to remain silent.

We would have to learn from the angels whose language is silence, interrupted only for praise. It can be only silence. Angels cannot say 'no' to God, because they love him too much. They do not tell him 'yes', because this is already understood. Instead of saying words, they simply do what he commands.

Christians have to speak, but they must also know when to be silent.

Now I realise that many of my prison dreams were only fantasies. I did not know the facts. I did not know that for all practical purposes the universal Church has almost no missionary work. If all evangelical missionaries were to abandon their fields and work only in China, there would be only one missionary for one hundred thousand people. I did not know this then. How could I have guessed that 94 per cent of the world's preachers speak to the 9 per cent of the world's population who are privileged to have English as their language, and only 6 per cent of the preachers witness to the 91 per cent who speak languages other than English?

I thought about establishing a mission to the Communist world. But our activity would prove to be much broader: it would consist in encouraging the Church to become missionary-minded, or, stated in another way, to really love Jesus and all mankind.

Two billion people do not know the holy name which is above every other name. Hundreds of millions have never heard about him, or, even worse, have heard a distorted message which has caused them to turn away from him.

The greatest gift any one can give his fellow-man is the concept of eternal life with its unlimited possibilities. Inspired by this understanding, men no longer melancholically count their years as steps towards death. Instead of counting years, they can have years which count.

A great task stood before me.

In any case, the setting of the sun does not cease when the sun crosses the horizon. The sentencing of Wurmbrand to twenty-five years hard labour was not the end of Wurmbrand. Caterpillars are said to mourn in the belief that when one has disappeared from among them it has died. A butterfly which flutters over the funeral service they have organised may be the former caterpillar for whom they grieve.

To forget the martyrs is to forget Christ

The relationship between Jesus and a believing soul is unique and cannot be fully explained in words because there are no terms of comparison. Let me try to find some metaphors. In a transfusion the blood of one man becomes another man's blood. If the latter man is injured and loses blood shortly after the transfusion, it is not the donor's but the recipient's blood that is lost. The donor's blood has become his own. After a heart transplant the heart belongs no longer to one man but to another. Similarly, between Jesus and the believing soul a transfusion, a transplant, a change in identity takes place.

Luther puts it like this: 'The Father tells Christ, "You become Peter who denies, Saul who persecutes, Judas who betrays, Magdalene who sins." Then the law sees Jesus full of all these offences and sentences him to death. Jesus has become the greatest murderer, thief, liar, adulterer whom mankind has ever known, not in the sense that he committed these crimes, but that he appropriated them to himself.' He becomes my sinning self. In exchange, he gives me his righteous identity. In his commentary on the Epistle to the Galatians, Luther daringly says: 'The Christian is Christ.'

He stands here on biblical ground. The greatest teachers of Christianity have taught this. St Ignatius writes, 'Christ is our inseparable life.' St Thomas Aquinas says that Christ and the Christians are 'quasi one mystical person'. The Scottish Catechism teaches: 'Christ is not another person from his people properly.'

A minister had tried unsuccessfully to bring faith to a great railroad trade union leader. A strike broke out. The strikers tightened their belts and held to their demands in the face of hunger and mounting debts. The strike went on. The minister went to see the trade union leader and told him, 'I have a suggestion which will enable you to win the strike and get the full weight of public opinion behind you.' The leader asked to hear the proposal. The minister explained, 'To demonstrate the truly desperate condition of the workers, and to arouse compassion for them, tie your son to a railroad track and have a locomotive run over him. This would ensure you the victory.' The trade leader was indignant. 'I would prefer to see the whole world starve rather than sacrifice my only son,' he said. At that point the minister was able to show him the love and wisdom of God which surpasses that of human leaders. God won over men of all nations, races, and social positions by sacrificing his only son.

God could have sent a saint of old or an angel to die for us, but instead he gave the best in heaven, Jesus Christ. Realising the extent of the sacrifice, our hearts are attracted to repentance. Jesus died for our sins on Good Friday, but death could not hold him. Death is a low quality phenomenon. It cannot contain the best. Jesus rose from death. This is what we celebrate on Easter Sunday: Christ conquering death.

God gave the best he had. Around me in other prison cells were saints of God who also gave their best, offerings of the finest flour as commanded in Leviticus 6:20. Some survived. Many died.

I dreamt that they would not be forgotten. To forget them is to forget the Lord, because the suffering Christians are not separate from Christ himself. Through them, he himself again suffers chains and persecution and torture in his mystical body, the church.

Westerners visit Eastern Europe

At the same time, other Christians abroad were preparing for the fulfillment of the same dream. They did not become co-workers, friends and contributors to the Underground Church simply as a result of the challenge I gave on my release. Books and sermons do not have the magic power we attribute to them as engineers of souls or makers of public opinion. Like news media, they merely strengthen existing tendencies. Years of Communist brainwashing of Hungarians and Czechoslovakians did not produce the desired result: the people rose in revolt at the first opportunity. Human life has its way; not determined by the media, but influenced by it to a certain extent. My challenge was received because souls in the West, ordained as children of God before the creation of the world, had been spiritually prepared for this new work they were to embrace.

In June 1964 I was released because of a general amnesty, having served fourteen years of my twenty-five-year sentence. I was then free within the greater confines of a jail called the Communist world.

I came into contact with two different Christian worlds. On the one hand there were delegations of distinguished bishops and Protestant pastors from the West. Some of them inquired specifically about me and gave substantial help to my impoverished family, but were not at all interested in hearing the full story of oppression. They never questioned me about it. When they preached, they weighed every word so as not to upset the Communists who hosted them. The attitudes of the Western leaders of the major Christian denominations towards Communism were similar to those of our own Romanian official church leaders, Orthodox or Protestant, who had compromised with the Reds.

There was nothing intrinsically wrong with this. During all church history, Christian leaders have taken contradictory attitudes in times of persecution. All had to resolve for themselves the questions: 'Is it wisest to allow the wolves, when they are so numerous and strong, to devour the sheep and the shepherds? Is it wisest to die heroically and have the whole church destroyed at the same time? Would it not be wiser to howl with the wolves, to let them believe we belong to them, and to make it possible for at least some of the church structure to survive?' So many Christian leaders chose to simulate friendship with the enemy. I can guarantee that the late Patriarch Justinian of Romania and the late Lutheran bishops Muller and Argay were not traitors, their intentions were the best. So were the intentions of many Baptist, Pentecostal and other official pastors.

Western church leaders who must deal with the Communists have the same calling from God. He looks to their hearts and if their intentions are pure, they will receive their just reward as surely as those who choose the way of martyrdom.

I have no doubt that some of the official church leaders from abroad had very open eyes, but many were fooled. They were shown a false Russia, a false Romania, a false Red China. They saw a Communist country as it looks when you are visiting it on a tourist visa.

But, as they were visiting a world which was one-third dominated by Communists, why should they not learn the Communist doctrine as it was proclaimed? Had they read *Voprosi Filosofii* (Questions of Philosophy), it would have become clear to them that there can be no religious liberty in a Communist country, even though it appears to exist. Here is an example taken from this Soviet magazine: 'From the point of view of Marxism-Leninism, freedom of conscience

. . . demands full denial of religion, its definitive defeat and its exclusion from social life.'

At that time I did not know that some Western church leaders worked for Communism with as much servility as many of our official Romanian bishops, priests and pastors. I realised only that they were compromising with the children of darkness.

On the other hand, not everyone is made for compromise. Everyone has his own calling. I sided with those who confronted the Communists headlong at the risk of losing everything. I did not believe them to be better than those who compromised, for we are all strangers in this world. I had to decide my position without judging others. I had been in Communist prisons and had seen the dark side of Marxism as those who had remained outside had not. I could not compromise.

Church leaders from abroad were allowed to preach. They had been naive enough not to bring their own translators with them. They preached with great care not to offend, but even their mild speech was not conveyed to the listeners as delivered. The translators, graciously engaged by the Communist-infiltrated Romanian churches, said whatever they pleased.

The visiting Christian leaders were shown only rosy pictures. None of them visited a prison or even asked to see one. I wondered why. Years later when I was in South Africa, I asked to visit the imprisoned Communists and was allowed to do so. In many other countries I have gone to the jails to see how criminals are treated. Church leaders who go to the East never visit prisons to see how their brethren in faith fare. They never ask for such permission.

I knew that through their compromises they might obtain some small concessions, each one valuable for the oppressed Christians. But I could not feel at home with them. They paid too much for these concessions. The church loses its credibility as a pillar of the eternal truth.

Time passed and we got another series of visitors from the West. This time the Communists did not allow them to preach. Discreetly word was passed around in Bucharest that an English and an American pastor would attend services the following Sunday in some Baptist churches.

They had to sit quietly in the pew. The authorities had forbidden them to open their mouths, as if they feared there might be dynamite in their words. They took some photographs of the congregation, but even this they were not supposed to do. They were permitted to give a Bible to every student of the Baptist seminary, but after they left the Bibles were confiscated. A student managed to slip a piece of paper into the English pastor's hands with the text 'Think on me when it shall be well with thee' (Gen. 40:14).

One afternoon I went to the German-speaking Baptist church. The English Pastor Stuart Harris, Director of the European Christian Mission and later also of the British Mission to the Communist World, was there. With him was brother John Moseley, who was then working for the USA Mission to Europe's Millions. They had heard about me. They had been looking for me but had not dared to ask anyone.

After the service I introduced myself to them in English. Looking around, I saw that we were surrounded by informers although fortunately none of them knew English. I invited Stuart Harris and John Moseley to my home. I could not give my address directly as this would have been understood by the informers. So I pronounced the letters constituting the name of the street one by one, with intervals. Later that night they came to the attic where we lived at the time. We met again the next day. I told them what was happening with the Christians in Communist countries. The dream to do something to help the persecuted saints was no longer only one man's dream; it was now a shared dream.

Other foreign visitors followed. One afternoon my wife awoke me from a nap. Five youngsters, American, Swiss and British, from an organisation called Operation Mobilisation, were there. From then on they brought us Bibles smuggled through customs. Little by little the knowledge about the persecution and the need to do something about it spread in small circles in the West.

On 6 December, 1965, my wife, my son and I were able to leave Romania. It was the feast day of St Nicholas, the patron of prisons for the Orthodox Church.

A ransom of £5,000 had been paid for us by the

Norwegian Israel Mission, the Hebrew Christian Alliance and my family. Communist countries practice slave trade. They sell their citizens like cattle. An old friend, Mrs Anutza Moise, struck the deal for us with the Romanian authorities.

2: To the West

In beautiful Norway

We went first to Italy where I was able to get in touch with the Lutheran World Federation whose headquarters were in Geneva. Then we went to Paris for a few days.

From there the Wurmbrand trio – my wife, my son Mihai and I – went to Norway. I did not know yet that cables warning everyone against having me preach had arrived ahead of us. The intentions were good: the Lutheran World Federation feared that my speaking out against Communism might make things worse for those left behind and might hinder any possibility of ransoming others in the future.

These fears proved futile. Everybody acknowledged that no one suffered in Romania as a result of my sermons and publication of my books, but that on the contrary, the Romanian Communists allowed the printing of Bibles for the first time, and today the number of imprisoned Christians is very small. We know of cases of Christians who were acquitted as a direct result of pressure exerted by our mission.

But for the time being the Lutheran church leaders from Geneva were playing the role of Moses who said to the Jewish people at the Red Sea, 'Stand still, and see the salvation of the Lord' (Ex. 14:13). But God said to Moses, 'Speak unto the [Jewish people] that they go forward,' and expected Moses not to wait and see but to do something himself – to lift up his rod and to stretch out his hand over the sea and divide it (Ex. 14:15, 16).

How should I speak out in spite of the ban? The Norwegian Israel Mission, which had paid most of our ransom, sent us to an extremely quiet rest home. Although their motive was kindness, the quiet solitude of that vacation home reminded me of the silence I had endured in solitary confinement. I wanted to speak and to write. I wanted to shout from the rooftops about the beauty of the

Underground Church.

Even today, but more so then, I dream that I am in prison almost every night. I don't believe that I dream about people who in reality are far away – I believe that real beings appear in dreams, just as the angel appeared to Joseph in his dream (Matt. 1:20). The underworld of jails, with its heroes, those who have been broken, those who die singing and those who have become informers, appears to me nightly. They all expect me to help them.

At 5 a.m. when everyone else is asleep, I awake with my brethren and sisters who are awakened by the gong – the signal that the slaves have to start working, the millions of slaves from the Chinese Ocean to the Baltic Sea and the Danube.

Prisoners' dreams are beautiful. All night long you are with your beloved; you eat luxuriously; you rejoice in reading the Bible and being in church. But the hammer beats on the rail. The slaves awake: pale, dirty 'skeletons' with dark circles around their eyes and hollow cheeks, afraid to look at each other because of their ugliness. They will have to labour, hungry and beaten, sometimes knee-deep in snow, sometimes in burning heat.

I am with them.

I am also with the Christians committed to asylums. The fact that these sane men pray is considered a sign of madness, and they are tied up, gagged, kicked and given electric shocks which will drive them mad.

The beauty of the underground saints shines against this dark background.

Knowing the cost, Brother Borushko told the court defiantly, 'Suffering is the living nerve of Christianity. The Church lives as long as it suffers, because Christ the Lord suffered martyrdom, and has asked us to follow Him.' Another Christian, Brother Krasnov-Levitin, wrote after eight years of imprisonment, 'Never and nowhere have I felt happier than in the prison camp . . . God was so near. In those times I asked, "My God, make this time, the brightest time in my life, last as long as possible." . . . So I found my felicity in unhappiness, and my inner liberty in the worst of captivities.'

I felt the urge to relate the story of a Christian child. An atheist reporter asked her, 'Do you look at books with pictures in them?'

She answered, 'Yes, books in which there are pictures of how our God suffered. He suffered for me, for you, for all men.'

When the reporter offered her a book, she refused it saying, 'It was written by godless men.'

'Your shoes too were made by atheists, and yet you wear them.'

'Then take them. I will walk barefooted, like my God.'

'You will get cold. It is unpleasant to walk barefooted.'

The child answered, 'May be. My God suffered and taught us to suffer.'

I could not stay silent.

By an error of omission, the American church in Oslo had not been warned by the Lutheran World Federation. So that was the first church I went to. On Christmas day, 1965, its pastor, the Rev Myrus Knutson, heard that a strange fellow had attended the children's Sunday school. He was a shabbily dressed man with a haggard look, probably an escapee from a prison or an asylum. Moreover, when he heard the story of Jesus told to the children, he wept. Who ever heard of someone weeping about the crucifixion in a decent church?

Pastor Knutson summoned me to his office and asked me to tell him my story. He showed immediate interest and the next day went to the headquarters of the Norwegian Israel Mission to find out if the story told by this Wurmbrand, that he had spent fourteen years in a Communist prison, was true. It was confirmed. He then asked to see a picture of me. There was one on the wall, but it did not resemble me at all. I had changed so much. Pastor Knutson persisted and met people who could identify me. Then he checked the story in Romania through the connections he had at the US Embassy. The reply from my homeland was conclusive.

At that time the first pulpit of a church in the free world was placed at my disposal and I preached there every Sunday. I also preached at the American military chapel where the pastor was Colonel Cassius Sturdy.

Those who heard my first sermons became aware of something new happening, or rather something valuable from the past that was being revived.

St Paul had gone to Thessalonica to preach. The essence of his sermons was that 'Christ must needs have suffered' (Acts 17:3). His listeners commented rightly that this meant '[turning] the world upside down' (v. 6). The Jews expected the Messiah to be the best of beings, a messenger from heaven who would make righteousness triumphant on earth, creating something like an ideal United Nations organisation, World Council of Churches, or Vatican, made up of all those who believed in the social Gospel, in the slow advance of humanism!

Long before Bonhoeffer, the Jews believed that mankind had matured to the point that it would surely embrace such a lovely being.

'No,' said Paul, 'love and truth incarnate had to die. And like him, all those who follow him will have to endure persecution.'

I showed how persecution was already occurring in one-third of the world, and that the rest of the world is also threatened.

The perspective was gloomy. The church must needs *suffer* also. 'It was given to [the beast] to make war with the saints, and *to overcome* them' (Rev. 13.7). Their only hope is to share in Christ's experience, who after he suffered death, 'rose again from the dead'.

The congregations I spoke to were used to sermons about which they could say at the end of the service, 'I enjoyed it very much.' But they suffered during my preaching and were moved to tears.

Speaking about Christ's new sufferings in his mystical body, the church, I had to name who caused her to suffer. I named a political power. So began the first of the rumours which would continually increase: 'Wurmbrand preaches politics'.

The staff of the US embassy frequented the American church in Oslo. They were embarrassed. I could easily sympathise with them: nobody who does cobbling to provide his daily bread would choose the same task for a hobby. The profession of the staff of the US embassy was dealing with foreign politics; they wished none of that on Sundays.

Since then, this question has often been debated in

43

connection with my name. The Bible contains books which are entirely political, such as Obadiah and Esther. In Esther, the name of God is not even mentioned. True preaching embraces all spheres of life. Avoiding politics in sermons is wrong.

On the whole I was received exceptionally well.

The first mission is formed

One of the members of the American church in Oslo was an English lady, Jill Holby. She introduced me to the family of a university lecturer, Vemund Skard, and arranged a party with them and with other people, one of whom was Over-bye, a retired journalist. Both the Skards and Overbye were determined people. They joined in action, telephoned the bishop of Tromsø, Monrad Norderval, a prolific author, and told him, 'We have here Richard Wurmbrand from Romania. The Norwegian churches are not open to him. The pastors have been told he might turn the world upside-down.' Norderval's reply was, 'Send him to me.' So we went up to the Arctic Circle. The cathedral of Tromsø was the first Norwegian Lutheran church in which I preached, followed by 'Filadelphia', the great cathedral of Norwegian Pentecostalism. The ban had been broken, and most other Lutheran cathedrals opened their doors. The Norwegian Mission behind the Iron Curtain was formed. It was the first organisation in Western Europe with a programme to help Christians under Communist oppression.

As to sister Holby who had arranged the party, she was at once rewarded by God. Up to this time her four-year-old son had had difficulty in pronouncing the simplest words. Now he began to speak. He could even say, 'Richard Wurmbrand, hallelujah!'. The day before, 'Good morning' would have been too difficult for him.

The press became involved in our cause. The interviews produced sensations. As time went by, there was scarcely a newspaper that did not publish pictures and articles about the atrocities committed against Christians in the Communist camp.

I was invited to speak to the NATO staff. NATO does not exist for the purpose of preaching the Gospel. As a matter of fact, it has no ideology, whereas the Communist officials who signed the Warsaw pact have a very definite doctrine which they wish to implant throughout the world. I simply told the NATO staff the story of Communism in Romania, the persecution and the Underground Church.

During the question and answer session, a high-ranking USA officer asked me why a peaceful co-existence between the two systems would be impossible. Since I was standing close to him, I made use of my years of experience living with pickpockets, and calmly snatched his wallet. Showing it to him, I asked, 'Are you now for peaceful co-existence with me?'

'Give me back my wallet.'

'Then you have the answer to your question.'

It might be argued that gangsters have nothing against the police; they only wish to keep whatever they have stolen. Were they allowed to do so, they would never harm a policeman. When gangsters get rich they become very generous, giving big tips to waiters, expensive gifts to friends, and even contributing to charitable organisations. They would gladly promote peaceful co-existence with the police.

These 'peace-loving gangsters' can be likened to the Communist regimes. Red China took over Tibet with a savage hand. 'Common tortures used by the Chinese are to compel men to stand naked and pelt them with stones, or to make them eat human excrement. Other atrocities include burying alive or using the prisoners for target practice. Buddhist monks are made to crawl like animals for reciting their sacred prayer, *Om Mane padme hum* (from *The Tibetan News Agency*, July 1975).

Red China covets the whole of Asia; the Soviet Union has enslaved half of Western Europe as well as portions of Africa. Otherwise the Communists are for peaceful co-existence. On the condition, of course, that they will not be required to give back what they have stolen.

The NATO officers took a collection for the purpose of sending my wife and me to the United States. Mihai, my son, who could not complete his studies in Romania because he had committed the crime of choosing the wrong parents, had other plans: he wanted to take his Bachelor

45

of Divinity at the Lutheran Theological Seminary in Paris.

But the trip to the United States was still far away. Pastor Knutson had to spend a lot of time organising my first schedule there.

I was very impressed by Norway. Pastor Solheim, my former colleague at the Norwegian Lutheran Mission to the Jews in Bucharest, had once told me, 'Norway is the most beautiful country in the world.' I had objected. 'This assertion is unbiblical. Palestine is declared by Moses to be the finest.' To which Solheim had replied, 'Yes, but Moses had not seen Norway.' Now I agreed with him.

I also have a high opinion of the Norwegians' Christianity. All German Lutheran bishops without exception had shouted 'Heil Hitler.' None of the Norwegian Lutheran bishops did so. With few exceptions, its whole clergy took a courageous stand against Nazism, even though this meant prison. The synod of the Norwegian Lutheran Church was the first great church body to protest against Communist persecution. The Norwegian Parliament was the first in the world to pass a resolution to that effect.

I spent many beautiful hours in the Norwegian churches. The Norwegian congregations are the only ones in the world who have as many missionaries abroad as they have pastors at home.

British problems

Next we went to Britain. There we met the Harris family which began secret missionary work in Communist countries as a branch of the European Christian Mission. As our outreach extended to China and other Communist countries, the Rev Stuart Harris founded the British Christian Mission to the Communist World.

Initially we held meetings in a small Baptist church after the evening service. As we grew, we met in larger churches and in cathedrals, at a large youth convention at Filey, and finally at the Royal Albert Hall – the most prestigious hall in London.

The English had a spiritual empire before they had a political one. Then Britain experienced a spiritual backsliding which was the result of a long process. St Willerbrord, an Englishman, introduced Christianity to the

Netherlands from where St Ansgar took it to Sweden. St Patrick, another Englishman, took Christ to the Irish. St Boniface, an Englishman too, felled the sacred oak of the Teutons and spread the Gospel among them.

Britain brought a good third of the world under its political power, and Englishmen caused the Gospel to triumph in the New World. Today the faith of most African, Asian, or Australian Christians is either the result of evangelisation by British missionaries or of the reading of the Scriptures which have been provided by the British Bible Society.

At the time I went to prison, the British empire was still intact. At the time of my release I discovered that the British had been the gravediggers of their own empire – they had given their colonies independence. As a result, there were countries on the map which I had never heard of before: Tanzania, Zambia, Pakistan, Malaysia. Today thirty-one African countries are dictatorships, seven of them governed by Communists. There had certainly been injustices in India when it belonged to the British, but since independence, millions of people have been slaughtered merely because they were Moslem or Hindu, Bengali or Bihari. Such slaughter would not have occurred under British rule.

The English are an imperial nation and will never be content without an empire. They must return to the time when Britain was a bastion of Christianity and liberty. Then God's light will shine again from the British Isles where, says some legend, Jesus trod as a boy. If Britain does not reinstate her Christian ideal, she is doomed to fall victim to the Communist ideal. I shudder when I think of the horrors this will bring. It is the privilege of the British Mission to the Communist World to make people conscious of this.

Britain is in a deep crisis but she is inhabited by a strange race. They are magnificent in crises, as World War II proved. The only time a British sailor fully shows what he can do is when his ship sinks. Britain will overcome her sickness.

Scenes from the Underground Church

British Christians, like those of other countries, listened with great sympathy when I spoke to them about the martyred Church. I quoted the description of such a church from a book written by an atheist lecturer, Klibanov. After an underground church meeting, the pastor asked Klibanov, 'How many people do you estimate were present today?'

Klibanov said, 'Approximately one hundred.'

'You are not part of us,' the pastor replied. 'If you were a Christian, you would know that we are one. Whenever Christians meet, two or three, hundreds or thousands, they are always one. You do not have the right vision. Were you to feel this sense of oneness for one moment, you would leave everything and unite with us.'

No one could have described the Underground Church more beautifully. This atheist's words remind me of the scripture in the Acts of the Apostles – that the first Christians were 'one soul and one heart'.

I told my British audience about an underground church in Russia which intended to baptise a number of Christians. This was forbidden and could result in imprisonment. After much deliberation, the Christians decided to perform the baptism at a fish nursery at the edge of town. They had been told that there was only one caretaker, and that he went to bed early.

The morning after the baptism, the caretaker went to the president of the local soviet: 'Comrade, give me a new job. I am not going back to the fish nursery. It is haunted.'

'What is this foolish talk? Communists are not superstitious. There is no such thing as haunted places.'

'I have to believe my eyes. Last night I saw some thirty beings dressed in white. They looked like men and women, but surely they did not belong to this earth. In the moonlight you could see an unusual goodness and meekness on their faces. They sang unearthly songs. You and I sing in the pub when we are drunk. But I assure you that these songs were quite different. I don't know what they had been drinking. One of them spoke aloud. It was in our language, but I could not understand it. Then they were all immersed in the water one by one. When they emerged from the water, their faces shone. I am sure that they were beings from another planet. I am frightened. So I will not go back to the fish nursery.'

I also recounted the words of a Christian who had just

been sentenced to death: 'I have welcomed all my bodily shapes. I was very happy as an infant. I was happy to have the body of a child; I was happy as a youngster; I was happy with the perfected body of a mature man. Should I not also welcome it when the body takes the shape of a skeleton?'

The last words of another Christian sentenced to death were: 'To die means to go out one door and to enter through another.'

British Christians took such teachings earnestly. Our mission in Britain had a good start.

My first encounter with the USA

I travelled to New York by ship. My wife and son followed later.

American Christians surpass European Christians in church attendance: 41 per cent of the population in America are churchgoers compared to only 1 per cent in Denmark and West Berlin and 2 to 5 per cent in other parts of Western Europe. No one should ridicule people who are merely churchgoers. Attending church is a genuine Christian witness for the timid believer. Not everyone is an extrovert; not everyone speaks easily for Christ; not everyone is a fighter.

Nor are we justified in sneering at nominal Christians. Should a nominal Christian wish to return to walking with the Lord, he knows the name to call upon. Men return to God in Turkey, but because there is no nominal Christianity they become faithful Moslems. After over one hundred years of Christian missionary activity in Turkey there are not even one hundred Christians there. Those who know how difficult it is to bring pagans to salvation will agree that even a nominal Christianity makes conversion easier; thus it should not be despised.

Secondly, American Christians provide 80 per cent of the world mission finances and 60 per cent of the world's missionaries. This does not correspond to the distribution of wealth and population of Christians in the world. The percentage given by Americans for missionary purposes is very low as such, but high in comparison to that of other rich nations.

I was impressed by the wealth in the United States. It

looked to me as though everyone was a millionaire. I had never owned a bicycle: in the USA even the simplest labourer might have a car, sometimes two. In supermarkets I would walk from one stand to another and say to myself, 'I don't need this; I don't need that.' Out of 100 items on the shelves, 99 seemed unnecessary. But people are not confined to only living with necessities. We could classify Beethoven and Leonardo da Vinci unnecessary – mankind could do without them. The majority of people in the world have never read St Thomas Aquinas or Kant, yet they have interesting lives. God gave the Americans wealth. Let them enjoy it.

I do not agree with an evangelist who, in reply to my appeal for something to be done to help the martyred Christians, wrote to me that he had another fight to lead: that against the devil of affluence. I could not understand how such a fight could be waged from affluent houses. Anyone who considers affluence to be of the devil should become like St Francis of Assisi and renounce riches. As for me, I believe that richness and poverty are spiritually neutral. Either can be consecrated to God or used by the devil. The rich Bossuet, who felt at home only in kingly palaces, is an ornament of the Church as much as a Christian who spent his life in ascetic practice.

But there are certain deplorable aspects to American wealth.

A survey showed that in Tuscon, Arizona, a town of 450,000 inhabitants, 9,500 pounds of perfectly edible food is thrown away annually – uncooked steaks, apples with one bite taken, cartons of eggs with brown shells instead of white, etc.

In Canada thousands of pounds of haddock are dumped overboard or put through ships' grinders as trash. Some ships dump 100,000 pounds on one trip. This because of some international fishing quotas regarding haddock.

In Ethiopia I saw hungry people walking miles to get one slice of bread and one cup of tea with sugar per day which was distributed by valiant Swedish missionaries. Were they consulted when the quotas were established in Canada?

The endless division among American Christian denominations also puzzled me greatly. We had no such thing in my homeland. Americans have six different Lutheran synods, scores of Baptist and Pentecostal denominations, United and disunited Presbyterians, Episcopalians, Reformed Episcopalians and Orthodox Episcopalians, etc. By having so many denominations to choose from, people tend to seek out a congregation which affirms their own views. In many cases a less comfortable choice might more effectively combat their sinful inclinations and show them the road to holiness which is not in accord with their present habits.

Fundamentalism and Modernism

Within both Protestantism and Catholicism in the USA there is a great controversy between fundamentalism and modernism.

I had never heard the word 'fundamentalism' in Romania. The first time I heard it was during a question and answer session in the USA when I was asked, 'Are you a fundamentalist?'

I answered, 'No.'

I thought that fundamentalism was one of many new cults. Later on, I was actually blackmailed by someone who said he would use this tape-recorded assertion against me. I told him, 'Just go ahead.'

Now I understand these terms.

Western fundamentalists seem to me not fundamental enough. They believe in the verbal inspiration of the whole Bible, yet few of them can read the original texts of the Bible. But this is not enough to be truly fundamentalist. The Hebrew text is not meant to be merely read, but chanted. Every word in the Hebrew text is composed not only of consonants and vowels but also of musical notes. A word which appears in different contexts is marked with different notes, which produces a variety of resonances in our hearts. Words of a hymn sung in a minor key do not produce the same result in our hearts as those sung in a major key.

When the Wycliffe translators studied the Mazatec tribe in Mexico they found that each syllable of the native language could be spoken on a different pitch or sequence of pitches. By changing the tone, a word might change from 'water' to 'cactus', or from 'trousers' to 'leaf'. Biblical Hebrew is also a tone language except that pitch does not change the meaning of the Hebrew word; but it modifies the communication to our souls of the reality clothed in a word.

One who does not know the tones cannot perceive the complete message of the Bible.

When St Paul wrote in Colossians 3:16 that we should admonish one another in hymns and spiritual songs, he meant though songs with specific tunes.

Music has great influence on the condition of the human heart. Those who suffer from sleeplessness do not need jazz music but children's songs. Fear can vanish through listening to Brahms' First Symphony or to 'A Mighty Fortress Is Our God'. Nervous irritations can be remedied through listening to the William Tell Overture, to Rossini, or to 'Jesus, Lover of My Soul'. A weary soul may be revived by Beethoven's 'Appassionata' or 'Stand Up, Stand Up for Jesus'. Music therapy has been introduced in hospitals to treat various emotional conditions.

The choice of the Hebrew notes, like the appropriateness of a musical style, depends upon the nature of the message as well as upon the nature, environment, or condition of the listeners.

The name Jehovah sung on the notes 'zirka', 'segol' or 'munach', the names of ancient Hebrew notes, has a differing effect on the soul, just as a classical chorale of the church has a different effect to a negro spiritual.

In Numbers 8:16 God said, '[The Levites] are wholly given unto me.' The literal translation from the Hebrew text would be, 'The Levites are given, given unto me' (*netunim, netunim*). This word is repeated but on different notes, which suggests that the Levites are given for the ordinary service of the tabernacle as well as, in the highest sense, to make atonement for sins.

Christianity must become much more Jewish and much more musical to be fundamentalist in the true sense of the word.

The fact that a multitude of varying texts exists shows the Bible to be the Word of God. Any atomic scientist will assert that reality is not fixed but is an undeterminable wave of probabilities. Every man we meet is likewise a cluster of probabilities. Because the Bible is the most perfect expression of reality, it must be based on texts that have many variations that are susceptible to many interpretations. Therefore, many Hebrew texts are ambiguous. For example, in Leviticus 5:19, the Hebrew *Ashom asham la-Jehovah* can be translated 'He is certainly guilty before the Lord', or, 'He has made complete restitution to the Lord'. God confronts us with different possibilities in order to stimulate our minds.

But these are only theoretical considerations regarding fundamentalism. Fundamentalist churches became our best friends. They believe the Bible; many of them live it. They know what it means to weep with those who weep. When they heard about those in bonds for Christ's sake, they felt the chains as their own and readily helped our missions.

On the other hand, the modernists were not modern enough for me.

Since the rise of biblical criticism, theological thinking has neglected an essential factor in religion: common sense.

A liar has no interest in inventing stories which are contrary to his interests and desires. The Jews claimed Palestine as their land. Even now they insist that it is rightfully theirs. Why would they invent the claim that they had conquered Palestine in a ruthless war with other peoples who had possessed it for centuries?

A liar will try to prove that he is from high lineage. The writers of the Jewish Scriptures could have no interest in inventing the fact that their kingly house had among its ancestors a professonal prostitute, Rahab, a loose woman, Tamar, and a member of a despised nation, Ruth the Moabite. No Nazi liar would have invented the story that Hitler's grandparents were Jews with the names of Abraham and Sarah. On the contrary, the German nation boasts that it stems from Siegfrieds and Parsifals. As for Jews, they say that they have been slaves for 400 years.

How stupid it would be on the part of the propagandists of a new religion to say that the Messiah they proclaim was born of a virgin, who had no husband, in a nation of no prestige, that the Messiah's own relatives considered him unbalanced, that his disciples never understood him, that he died among criminals, and that even his apostles

53

doubted his resurrection. The Bible talks about all these matters simply because this is how it happened.

It is not modern to leave out common sense when dealing with religion. Yet that is what the modernists do; therefore they are not modern.

But theology is not my real concern right now. I want to help those who are persecuted in Communist countries. All the modernists are involved with the World Council of Churches which supports, not the Christians martyred by the Reds, but Communist guerrillas. I could not go along with them.

I met the leading anti-Communist fighters of the United States and appreciated the good work they had done to expose Communism. I did not feel the call to become another militant. I felt that in this battle it is not so much militants as saints that are needed.

Western freedom

I rejoiced at being in a world where I had the freedom to speak, write and move around. It was so unlike life under Communist rule.

I wondered how long this tenuous freedom in the West would last. We had fled from Romania to the USA; where would we flee from here in the event of a Communist takeover?

America has freedom, but not a true democracy. In most of the democratic countries (except perhaps Scandinavia, Britain and Switzerland) the situation is the same.

For example, 97 per cent of Americans are not active in politics. Only half of those entitled to vote do so. They do not contribute anything to any political party – no money, no work at the polls, no attendance at precinct meetings, no volunteer service on behalf of any candidate. They sit back, allowing others to get the job done. This leaves the running of the government in the hands of 3 per cent of the population. Furthermore, Gallup polls found that 57 per cent of Americans cannot name their Congressman, and 81 per cent cannot cite a single thing he has done. Americans know far more about entertainers and football players than about their elected representatives.

Sad to say, such apathy and ignorance appear to be endemic among American evangelical Christians as well, although their forebears were among the leading builders of the American system. A survey of voting habits in Chicago during a recent four-year period showed that only 17 per cent of the Protestant ministers even bothered to go to the polls, while 99 per cent of the innkeepers cast ballots.

Why should we adhere to institutions that were formed when the US was an agricultural republic of three million inhabitants, institutions which are no longer suitable for a nuclear superpower threatened with annihilation by the Communists? I would rather support a government which granted freedom only to lovers of freedom. Lincoln did not hesitate to suspend the writ of habeas corpus during the Civil War because the acts of traitors made such a move imperative.

The West is subverted today by more traitors than the USA was in Lincoln's time. A law should be enacted which would make advocacy of Communism an act of treason against freedom. The only freedom given to Communists should be the freedom to emigrate to countries which have a regime they like. This should also apply to Fascists and racists of all colours and creeds.

Communism per se

Now we return to the story of how the mission Jesus to the Communist World was established in the United States.

I travelled from coast to coast preaching to packed Lutheran churches. I met with the president of one of the American Lutheran synods who received me cordially. For twenty minutes he told me about the religious liberties that had been obtained in Communist countries through the efforts of the World Council of Churches. He did not ask me even one question. Then it was another visitor's turn.

The president of another Lutheran synod was an exceptional man whose humility particularly impressed me. However, he believed that there is nothing objectionable in Communism *per se*, although putting it into practice is wrong. That is like saying that prostitution or alcoholism are alright so long as no one practises them. He also believed in the possibility of peaceful co-existence between the Christian Church and Communism. He had seen evidences of religious liberty on his visits to the East, but he did not realise how he had been misled. He was very kind to me, offering me a minor position in the Department of Evangelism of his church. However, his church did not really evangelise and the department has since been dissolved, so had I accepted the offer I would soon have become unemployed. Nonetheless, I remain grateful to this man who personally helped bring me out of Romania after hearing about me through a common friend.

As to Communism *per se*, this is reflected in the events in Cambodia, where at least one million people were killed when the Communists took over, among them all those who had any sort of education, including school children of twelve, and all active Buddhists and Christians. No bullets were squandered on them – their heads were simply smashed with sticks and shovels.

Jesuit priest F. Gomey, who spent fifteen years in Vietnam, reports that a high-ranking Communist official from Hanoi told him, 'We do not admit the heresy of pluralism because this means division and weakness. We care only about the people . . . People are only those who have the correct ideology and live according to it. There are some stubborn, hard-headed men like Archbishop Thuan [then in prison] who will never become people . . . Nobody will come out of the concentration camp until he is converted to Communism. Those who do not convert will disappear.'

When the priest asked about religious freedom under Communism, the official answered, 'Freedom exists so that you can obey the rules of the Party in various ways.' Shocked by the official's frankness, the Jesuit said, 'I am a foreigner who can leave the country. If I repeat these things in the free world, it will certainly be bad propaganda for Communism.' But the official replied, 'Priest, nobody will believe you.'

In Communist Ethiopia thousands of people were put to death without appearing before any court. Families could obtain the bodies of their loved ones for burial, but they had to pay for the bullets with which their relatives were shot: an official would count the wounds and they paid accordingly.

This is Communism *per se*. Communism with a human face as proclaimed by the Czech Communist Dubcek is either fantasy or clever propaganda. 'Eurocommunism' or democratic Communism is just a slogan whose intent is to deceive.

We do not expect the Communists to have a human face. In South-East Asia and Africa, wherever they are corrupt, we bribe them. A gift of only two hundred dollars can sometimes save a prisoner from death.

How I became known

In my speeches throughout the United States, I insisted again and again that the Church should have a specific budget to help the families of Christian martyrs, and that she should propagate the Gospel behind the Iron Curtain. Long exchanges of letters followed which ended when the head of one of the denominations told me the conclusion to which he had arrived: that my reason was blurred and my mind confused.

No doubt he was right in this diagnosis. No one who endured many years of Nazi and Communist prisons and tortures can be completely sane. This was shown in a scientific survey of the victims of Auschwitz.

But the fact that my reason may be blurred cannot free those whose reason remains intact from the obligation to help their persecuted brethren in faith. But these men used my madness as an excuse for doing nothing.

Nonetheless, God has mysterious ways of doing things. If it was his will that our mission should exist, then somehow a way would open.

At this time I was in Philadelphia visiting some people who had shown interest in my message. Throughout the city posters announced an anti-Vietnam rally. I was curious. Because my English was poor, I stood near the speakers' platform in order to catch every word. At a certain point, a pastor wearing a clerical collar delivered a vehement speech against LBJ. I did not realise that the initials represented President Johnson's name, so I was not interested. Then he spoke for peace, and here I agreed. But when he concluded by praising Communism, I could no longer stand still. I burst onto the platform, pushing him aside easily as he was a much smaller man than myself. I grabbed the microphone and spoke into it: 'What do you know about Communism? I earned my doctorate in it. I can show you the diploma.' I undressed myself to the belt showing the scars on my body. 'These are the marks of Communist tortures.' The pastor asked me why I had been tortured. 'Suppose I was a murderer,' I said. 'Were Oswald or Ruby tortured? Should murderers be tortured?' People from the audience shouted, 'No, of course not.' I went on addressing them. 'I was never charged with murder. I was tortured for being a Christian. I am a clergyman like him. But he is a Judas. Instead of praising Christ and the martyrs, he praises the murderers.' Many booed him then, and some shouted, 'Judas'. Then someone cut the wire of the microphone and the meeting was called off.

Police surrounded me and escorted me out of the meeting. I had committed two illegal acts: I had undressed myself in a public place and I had disturbed a lawful meeting. But once we rounded the corner and were out of sight, the police shook my hand and congratulated me.

The following day my picture appeared on the front page of all the newspapers. One picture showed me surrounded by police and had the caption, 'If Kennedy had been guarded like this he would not have died.'

When news of what had happened in Philadelphia reached Washington, I was invited to testify before a US Senate sub-committee, I thought the meeting would be composed of a couple of senators. To my surprise, the room was filled with innumerable TV cameras, broadcasters, representatives of all the world news agencies, UPI, Associated Press, Reuters, etc. I became known throughout the world overnight. Invitations to preach and to lecture poured in; the record of my testimony became one of the Government printing house's bestsellers and was translated into many other languages. The publicity resulting from these events impelled me further along the road towards establishing the mission to the Communist world about which I had dreamt in prison.

3: The next step

But there was to be an intermezzo before this dream could be fulfilled. I had to become acquainted with commercialism in religion, a phenomenon relatively unknown in Western Europe and even less so behind the Iron Curtain, where the reward for preaching is prison or death. I had many unexpected experiences during this period.

When I received my first invitation to preach at a university and was asked what my honorarium would be, I answered, 'It is honour enough to preach the Gospel. I can't see why an honorarium is needed. Where I come from, the honorarium for telling the story of Christ is twenty-five years in prison. If you witness for him in jail, it is twenty-five sticks. I will speak without an honorarium.' The invitation was cancelled. I was considered a nut.

One Sunday I was to preach in Michigan. I was the guest of a family whose daughter was in high school. When this girl invited a friend to hear me speak, the friend replied, 'What? That idiot? You invited him? He preached in our church. I never heard anybody so stupid.' The daughter repeated this to her mother who became very embarrassed, not knowing any more how to treat me in case I really was an idiot.

The following Monday morning I had a speaking engagement at a businessmen's breakfast meeting. Before the meeting started the chairman came up to me accompanied by another man. 'Please don't feel offended,' he said. 'This gentleman says his name is Richard Wurmbrand and that he has spent fourteen years in Communist prisons. Here is a cheque from our church which he endorsed with the name of Wurmbrand. Please identify yourselves. We wish to find out who is the real Richard Wurmbrand.'

I showed my passport, but the other man had no identity

59

papers with him. Pressed further he finally acknowledged that his name was not Richard Wurmbrand. When I asked him why he had signed my name on the cheque, he replied, 'How do you know that I signed your name?'

'But here it is,' I said. 'You signed "Richard Wurmbrand".'

The man answered calmly. 'You are surely not the only Richard Wurmbrand in the world. I might have signed for somebody else with the same name.'

I liked his answer, but I went on, 'Did this other Richard Wurmbrand authorise you to sign his name?'

Again the man's reply was steady and calm. 'Did any other Richard Wurmbrand authorise you to investigate me?'

The police took him into custody but released him the same day. That evening he telephoned me with the following proposal.

'Say, America is a big country. You can't possibly tell your life story everywhere. I know it as well as you do. I've listened to tapes of your speeches and you can fill me in on some more details. Here's the deal. We can divide up the states and cover a lot more territory with two Richard Wurmbrands than you can with just one. The financial arrangement will naturally be, shall we say, highly beneficial to both of us.'

The man was astounded when I did not accept such a practical proposal.

I have compassion for such religious manipulators. They are victims of commercialised religion. One of them whom I came into conflict with told me the story of his life. He came from a broken family in which the children were carriers of lies from one parent to the other. He had been brought up in a church in which there had been many 'Hallelujahs', but little real teaching. In this unwholesome atmosphere, religions were promoted like competing brands of vacuum cleaners, and from an early age this man had observed money-pushing, money-grabbing and unabashed dishonesty from pastors. His religious teachers were far from being saints who could have inspired him with awe.

As a young man, he had somehow understood that Christian work in Communist countries could only be achieved through underground means. Unfortunately Americans would not support such activity. But he found that if he invented 400 non-existent missionaries and asked for money to support them, he would get it. It was as though Americans liked to be fooled. I remember him telling me once, 'The bigger the lie, the more easily it is believed.' Indeed, this often proves true and, prompted by good intentions, he acted according to this principle. I hold no grudge against him.

God helps us through our friends

When we started missionary work on our own, it was first as a department of the American branch of the European Christian Mission. This later became known as Jesus to the Communist World.

On 6 December, 1980, it was the fifteenth anniversary of our coming to the West; on 3 May, 1982, it was the fifteenth anniversary of the United States mission Jesus to the Communist World.

The clock and calendar record the passing of those fifteen years. The same implements measured my fourteen years in prison. But time is of various qualities. One American friend told me that the longest stretch of time he had ever lived was a five minute fire fight during World War II. He had been trying to stay hidden in a man-of-war. He emerged from this experience middle aged and so he remained, even though the calendar had recorded only one day in his life.

Nobody knows what time really is. Clocks and calendars can measure time only in quantity. They do not assess its quality. Time is of the essence, but the essence of what?

Ten years in the free world were no more equivalent to ten years in prison than the *pohod na Sibit* of Czarist times, when prisoners spent over a year journeying thousands of miles across Siberia on foot, is equal to an astronaut's experience of flying over the whole of Siberia in less than a second.

One day Toscanini is reported to have asked Einstein, 'Please explain the relativity of time you wrote about.' Einstein replied, 'We might speak about this at dinner. Until then, please explain a Mozart symphony to me.'

'You have to listen to it,' Toscanini said.

'Well,' replied Einstein, 'it is the same with the relativity of time. You have to live it.'

Jesus to the Communist World has been the fastest growing mission in the world. It expanded to include fifty countries. Its income during the first year was £50,000. Now it is over £3½ million.

Such rapid growth is due to many factors, not the least of which is the grace of having a family who worked wholeheartedly with me. My wife has laboured and travelled with me the whole time, preaching and often moving her audiences to tears.

In Genesis 22:6 it is written, 'Abraham and Isaac went together.' This is how it has been with my son Mihai and myself. Although he had been considered a poor assistant driver, he proved to be a good mission director. Working night and day, without ever taking vacations or days off, he took care of all administrative work. He helped establish missions on all continents, preached, and in the fifteen years since he came to the West he has also earned three degrees – in theology, psychology and law – so he has more than compensated for the lack of opportunity to study under Communism. He found a wife, an Israeli Christian, Judith, tailored especially for him. She is a confirmation of an old Talmudic story: 'In six days God created heaven and earth,' said one rabbi, 'and on the seventh, he rested.' 'What has he been doing since?' asked another. The first rabbi answered, 'He matches couples.' My son's marriage was just what he needed, a wife who, when she married him, married the mission too, demanding nothing for herself.

The second grace was finding a good editor for my books. I write in a language equivalent to that in which I think. Ellen Oblander corrects my rough and unorthodox English with a gentle touch coming from a gentle heart. My third grace was to find in Edward England my first publisher and a friend. My book *Tortured for Christ* has a circulation of millions of copies in 56 languages. Other books followed.

In Zimbabwe, a mother read parts of *Tortured for Christ* to her nine-year-old son. The boy wrote and asked me to organise a mission in Zimbabwe. He offered to lead it himself. I wrote the boy a lengthy reply, and soon afterwards his mother, Sister Ward, became our Zimbabwe director.

Some time later, I went to preach in Bulawayo, the second largest city of Zimbabwe. It was a big meeting, attended by both whites and blacks. The mayor of the city was a Jew. He came to welcome me, wearing a gold chain, a tradition dating back to the time when the country belonged to Britain. The meeting opened with the hymn, 'Ye Chosen Seed of Israel's Race, Ye Ransomed from the Fall'. It was clear that all the Christians there, black and white, considered themselves to be of Israel's race, though the mayor had assumed until then that only Jews belonged to this race. In his word of welcome he expressed his bewilderment. I had to explain things in my sermon.

At a meeting in Britain, I had met a South African brother, Pat Henegan, who showed great interest in the Christian work being done in Eastern Europe. He invited me to his country. At our first meeting in Johannesburg there were 15,000 people, and enormous rallies took place in other cities as well. I went back to South Africa many times. Henegan became the general secretary of a flourishing mission there. Our mission's newsletter has been published in twenty-three languages spoken by the African peoples, and my book *Tortured for Christ* was translated into Swahili and Shona.

At first the South African Mission was concerned only with Russia and Red China. But soon Communism came to South Africa's own borders. Great quantities of Christian literature were smuggled into Angola and Mozambique. Radio Mozambique protested that the river Enkomati was polluted with Christian 'counter-revolutionist' literature. It is our mission which was behind this.

When Holland was under Nazi occupation, the Dutch underground resistance chose one of their members to infiltrate the Gestapo under the pretence of being a collaborator. Gaining the Nazis' confidence, he was able to inform the Dutch resistance about many Nazi decisions and thus he saved many lives. When the Allies freed Holland, they imprisoned all Nazi collaborators and were not very careful about ascertaining who was working for whom. Thus this man spent many months being ill-treated in jail before he could prove his real allegiance. Finally he was rehabilitated and decorated and went on to become a pastor. But his innocent suffering left an indelible mark in his soul.

After reading *Tortured for Christ* he sent it immediately to his son-in-law in Canada, asking him to do something for the innocent sufferers in Russia. The son-in-law collaborated with some other people and created our mission in Canada. I have preached there often, in both Catholic and Anglican churches, as well as in free churches and universities. The Canadian mission is led by Nellie and Klaas Brobell.

The Dutch patriot did not create the mission in Holland because this had already been done by Brother Maris, who had translated my hearing before the United States Senate sub-committee into Dutch, and who also translated my other books later on. His wife, who has since gone to the Lord, helped him greatly in establishing a flourishing mission in Holland.

When Sister Coletta Grossu, one of my wife's companions in prison, was able to leave Romania with her husband, Sergiu, a fellow prisoner of mine, she became the director of our mission in France. Another friend who helped in this work was Alice Panaidor, who had cared for my son during our imprisonment and afterwards went to prison herself for five years. Together Coletta and Alice organised huge meetings in Paris and other cities. Enormous quantities of our books were distributed and much help went to Christians behind the Iron Curtain. Coletta also wrote a remarkable book, *Blessed Be Thou, Prison*.

I was advised not to start a mission in France. I was told that there were only Catholics and Communists in France, and that no one would support a Protestant mission. This warning did not prove true.

There are, in fact, very few Protestants in France. A recent Paris survey showed that only one person in seven could name one of the four Gospels, and only one in twenty-four had ever opened a Bible. Only 2 per cent of the French population claim any Protestant connection, and only 0.4 per cent can be considered Evangelical. But our mission's purpose was not to debate who was right, 400 years ago, when Protestants quarrelled with Catholics. Our aim was to help persecuted Christians – Protestant, Orthodox and Catholic. We did not alienate the rank-and-file Communist either – we tried to show him love. Today our mission in France is prospering.

A German missionary in Brazil, Brother Ostermoor, who received a copy of *Tortured for Christ* from relatives, now aged seventy-eight, leads our mission work in that country. When *Tortured for Christ* was translated into Portuguese, it received nation-wide television coverage in Brazil.

Brothers Newton and Umoru organised a vigorous mission in Nigeria. Missions arose in Zaire, Upper Volta, Benin, Zambia etc.

In Germany a group of nuns who had read *Tortured for Christ* at their daily devotions published one of my sermons and organised my first preaching schedule there. Then they read my second book, *In God's Underground*. This book shocked and frightened them. In it I recounted how I had unmasked a stool-pigeon in prison, a man whose denunciations had caused other prisoners, already ill with tuberculosis, to be forced to stand naked on freezing wet concrete in the dead of winter. I did not practise love with this informer, but outwitted him. In another case I showed how sometimes love takes precedence over the truth, and how I fooled an interrogator in order to save some brethren from arrest. These apparent contradictions must have confused the nuns because they cancelled my schedule, writing me an angry letter and sending warnings to others who had invited me to speak.

However, I preached in Germany nonetheless. Important people attended and some of them decided to establish a German mission. When we returned to the United States we were informed that a strange situation must have developed in Germany: mail was not being collected by the mission and was accumulating in the post office; and people who had contributed money were not receiving any receipts. Since we could not explain this, my wife returned to

Germany to speak with the president of the newly-formed mission. The director was not at home, but his wife told Sabina, 'The Communists can take over West Germany at any time and I do not want my husband hanged. I have forbidden him to become involved in these mission affairs.' Most German Christians had not been eager to stand up against Hitler's prohibitions, and now they could not even stand up to their wives. Other committee members had also lost their courage and given up their commitments.

Something had to be done. God sent us help from an unexpected quarter.

There was a small group of believers in Germany headed by a preacher named Fritz Braun who still believed that the sun turns around the earth, because that is what the Bible says. Like Luther, he did not accept Copernicus. He believed that heaven is directly above and hell below us. He also preached that the European nations belong to the ten lost tribes of Israel. Not many people listened to him, but he showed that his heart was in the right place.

The old Prussian order still reigned in the Brauns' home: sons were expected to obey their father even though they were forty years old. Fritz Braun simply ordered one of his sons, a factory owner, to drop everything and take over the mission. That is how it happened. The German mission has become the most prosperous European mission and has expanded to Austria, Switzerland, Italy, and West Africa. It is the centre of our activities in Communist Europe.

God and the devil use Switzerland in a special way. The Communist Party of Russia was created by Lenin in Switzerland. There together with other Russian dissident refugees, he plotted the revolution that overthrew the Russian Emperor, established Communist dictatorship, and expanded afterward to encompass one third of the world.

Zionism, the movement for re-establishing God's chosen people in Israel, also started in Switzerland.

In the same hall in Basel where Theodor Herzl, the founder of Zionism, had spoken at their first congress, I could speak for our Swiss mission. Our brother Hans Zurcher was among its founders. The mission publishes material in German, French and Italian, the three languages of Switzerland.

Giuseppe Laiso had been a sympathiser of Communism. After reading our books and learning the truth, he started our mission in Italy, eventually creating the radio station belonging to our International fellowship. Terrorists wrecked it.

Portugal has almost been taken over by the Communists. In the most difficult times, when standing up for Christ against Communism meant risking one's life, Brother Trancoso, our Portuguese director, maintained his mission quarter in Barera, the most Communist town of the country. Unafraid he published our literature under their noses.

I preached in Portugal in a hall in which men stood jammed so close together that when the Communists arrived late to beat me up, could not penetrate to the platform. To carry out their mission they first had to listen to my whole talk. This they did. Their desire to beat me passed.

Sister Hadinata organised our mission and published our books in Indonesia, a Moslem country.

I went to Ethiopia and Kenya, warning everyone who would listen about the impending Communist peril in Africa. In Addis Ababa I was received by the United States Ambassador and his wife who assured me that America was much admired by the Ethiopians. Clearly the Ambassador lived in a fool's paradise: within a year Ethiopia was ruled by the Communists. The Soviet Ambassador had not spent his time dreaming about friendship, but had worked concretely at taking over the country.

When I went to Ethiopia I also visited Asmara, the capital of Eritrea, and held a large student meeting there. The students' questions all showed their leftist tendencies. When they questioned me about South Africa, I told them that as long as the whites ruled, the black population of South Africa would be safe, that the whites would not exterminate the blacks. The danger would arise from within the black population because of rivalries amongst themselves. One year later extensive killing began in Eritrea. The Communist Ethiopean troops marched into Voki-Deva, an Eritrean village, one Sunday morning and shot all the people gathered in the church. Some time later in the United States I met a student who had attended my meeting in Asmara. He told me that my warning had been remembered for long afterwards.

Narajan Nair read my book *Tortured for Christ* while he was studying in Australia. Returning home to the Fiji Islands, he started a mission there, and poor natives now give money for their persecuted brethren in Communist countries.

The brethren Res Werry and Merv Knight of Australia were stimulated by the same book and started our mission on that continent.

In India, brother Job was greatly inspired by our literature. Although at that time India was a dictatorship, he organised huge meetings with as many as 80,000 people present at one time. Job now leads our Indian mission, printing books and newsletters in over twenty languages.

It is a miracle of God that this mission succeeded in a very short time in creating the second largest Christian printing shop of India, called Sabine Press, which provides literature not only for India, but also Nepal, Bhutan, Tibet, Sri Lanka, and other Asian countries. Since the cost of printing is cheaper in India than anywhere else, Sabine Press also produces our newsletters and books for Nigeria, Zambia, Zaire, Upper Volta, and other African countries. A substantial part of this tremendous expense is covered by the gifts of the poor Indian Christians, who have an average yearly income of £100. Our Indian Mission 'Love in Action' is the biggest branch in the International Christian Mission to the Communist World.

Brother Job is sustained in his work by a marvellous wife, a Protestant Mother Theresa. A doctor, she abandoned a well-paid position in a foreign hospital to serve without pay as a physician in the slums. Brother Pereira left a highly envied position in the Anglican cathedral to work for our mission in the slums of Sri Lanka.

It is almost unknown in the West that among the Federation of States that comprise India, until 1981, three were Communist-ruled: Kerala, Tripura and West Bengal. It was partly due to our activity in enlightening people about the real nature of Communism that the Communist government of Kerala could be replaced at the end of 1981, but two states are still Communist.

I had to preach in Alepi, a town nicknamed 'India's Moscow' because it is the center of Communist activities.

Some 30,000 people were gathered on open ground. The atmosphere was tense. At the very least much heckling was expected, but the Communists could resort to violence, too. We had not appealed for police protection.

At the very time when the meeting began, a heavy rain started. It rained all around the area where we had the meeting. No rain fell on our sacred ground. People were amazed. While Christians praised the Lord, their enemies were dumbfounded and kept silent.

In Malaysia brother Ronney Kon was working as a distributor of Christian literature. As he did not have time to read all of the books he handled, he distributed my book *Tortured for Christ* for several years before someone told him about its content and inspired him to read it. As a result a mission was formed.

Brother Kon arranged huge meetings for me in Kuala-Lumpur, Singapore and other oriental cities. Everywhere I had to adjust to the cultural and religious attitudes of my audience. In a Buddhist country I would sometimes start like this:

'I have great respect and admiration for Buddha and am happy to be among those who recognise his greatness. When I was very young I was impressed by a story which he told. Once there was a good prince who could not bear to see anyone suffer. One day he found a starving tigress in a wood, her cubs near her, doomed also to starvation because she had no milk for them. This was more than the prince could bear. Although the tigress might be cruel, she was still a living being and was included in his love. Cutting his veins to arouse her, he lay down near her to be devoured. The tigress ate him. New life entered her and she now had milk for her cubs. The prince had died, but wild creatures had been saved.

'As a boy I wondered whether this were only a fairy tale. I knew that men could be savage and cruel, but I had never met such a loving being as this prince. I admired Buddha for his story and I regretted that princes such as the one he described existed only in literature.

'After many years, someone gave me the Bible to read. There I found another story; that a Prince of Peace was born into the world. This Prince said to men who were as brutal as wild animals, and in danger of eternal death, "Eat my body, drink my blood, and you will live." These men killed him. Since that time the Church has fed on his sacrifice, and sinners are allowed to enjoy eternal life. The Prince died that the whole world, like the tigers of Buddha, might be saved.

'When I came to believe in Jesus, I did not forget the great oriental prophet who had had, six centuries before it was to happen, such a premonition of the Saviour who was to come.'

When I spoke in India I quoted from their Holy Scriptures and their wealth of myths. When I met Communists I would quote Marx, Lenin and Mao. This practice opened many souls to my message.

I am disturbed when our mission is referred to as 'Wurmbrand's Mission'. When I hear this it reminds me of the Epistle of Paul to Philemon which was written jointly by Paul and Timothy, although Timothy's contribution was ignored in the title of the epistle. Mission to the Communist World is the result of a common effort of numerous directors, scores of committee members, an international staff with various assignments in our offices on every continent, and thousands of contributors, broadcasters, couriers, printers, and prayer-partners. I apologise that I cannot mention all of them by name because of lack of space.

We begin the underground work

We began to make the existence of the Underground Church known all over the world, publicising Christian heroism like that of the Soviet Captain Gavrilov in fifty languages. This man was executed for organising a secret Christian Officers' Union, and for publishing its magazine. Two lieutenants were arrested with him. In the free world, officers simply ask themselves if it is their duty to join such a union, taking the freedom for granted. In England I was able to preach freely before the Military Academy at the invitation of the British Christian Officers' Union. In Russia, Christian officers relinquish their liberty for joining such a union.

As gifts poured in from many countries, we were able to

start helping this courageous Underground Church.

Antonio Borro, a Christian teacher from Cuba, who had been in prison there for his faith, told American audiences how Cuban prisoners were treated. He had been put in a cell, a kind of cage in which there was only enough room for him to sit. He was dragged by the feet to interrogations, beaten with ropes and sticks.

Prisoners there were put in acid baths, hammers and sickles were tattooed on their skin with red-hot pokers, and their heads were enclosed in boxes with live bees. While imprisoned, Borro was shown a picture of medical students practising vivisection on human beings. He was then threatened that this would happen to him too unless he confessed to having committed immoral acts, having been a CIA agent, and being an opponent of Communism. When he could endure no more, Borro 'confessed'. The only true part of his confession was that, like every Christian, he opposed Communism.

But few Cuban prisoners were fortunate enough to escape. A Baptist preacher named Rameiro died in prison because he refused to confess. The last words of a young man named Boitel who was shot by the Communists were, 'Long live Christ the King!'

Now, through our mission, we could help the families of such martyrs. Christian booklets were set afloat in strategic locations where the ocean currents would carry them into Cuban, Chinese, Korean, Albanian or Russian shores. We had thoroughly studied the currents, and we knew we could depend on the Lord for their constancy. We packed a Gospel or Bible portion in a small, vacuum-sealed plastic bag in which we had inserted a plastic straw to insure that they kept afloat. Inside we also placed a piece of candy or chewing gum which showed through the plastic and would arouse the interest of children as well as adults. This innovative idea was my son's, and we rejoiced at how well it worked.

Red China had been forgotten by the universal Church, yet God must love the Chinese people very much. The proof is that he made so many of them. Under Mao all the churches in Red China were closed. A million Christians there have been killed and seemingly the Church in the

West does not even bother to mention these Christian martyrs in prayer – names like Wen-Yuang, Kung, Liu-Ling-Chiu, Chou-Ching-Tse, Tung-Hu-En, Fang-Ai-Shih, Chou-Fu Ching, Marcus Cheng and thousands of others.

We reminded the universal Church about our suffering brethren in China and described how they were treated, according to information received from the office of the Dalai-Lama, the highest authority of the Buddhist religion. In inner Mongolia, Communists cut off the tongue of Lama Huh-Lu, a Buddhist monk. They cut off the fingers on both hands of a teacher, Saranchulu, and burnt alive the child of a woman named Nominerdene. Another teacher, Munk-bish, had his genitals and face burnt with a branding iron, and lost his reason as a result of this treatment. Damba, Dambaii and Dambalah were hanged from a tree by their thumbs and boiling water was poured over their heads.

Surely Christians are concerned when Buddhists are treated in this way. Our Christian brethren are enduring these horrors also. At last we had a world-wide mission which could help the families of these martyrs and make their cries heard in the easy-going free world.

Meeting apathy

I have travelled extensively on all continents, made innumerable TV and radio appearances, given interviews, delivered lectures and sermons, and written twelve books which have been widely translated and distributed.

I have often reminded my American audiences of the words preached by John Winthrop on the deck of the *Arabella* as she ploughed across the Atlantic to Massachusetts in 1630. 'We shall be as a city upon a hill,' he said, 'the eyes of all people upon us. If we shall deal falsely with our God in this work we have undertaken, and so cause him to withdraw his present help from us, we shall be made a story and a by-word throughout the world.'

Before German audiences I have dared to utter again 'fatherland', the word which had become taboo for them because Hitler had so abused it. Following the war, the German people swung to the opposite extreme and all but banned it from their vocabulary. Now I asked them, 'How can a Christian profess to love his enemies if he does not even love his own fatherland enough to do his utmost to free his compatriots who are under Communist oppression?' I referred to those in East Germany, separated from the West by the infamous Berlin Wall.

Everywhere I have met with enthusiastic support from children of God. But I have also met the devil called 'apathy'. This is an ancient devil indeed, who had sat with the people on the hill of Golgotha and said, 'Let be, let us see.'

Indifference and insensitivity to suffering are deeply embedded in human beings and are not peculiar to modern men. We sometimes wonder why people nowadays do not react when they are told the story of Christ on the cross, and why they remain unmoved when they hear about the sufferings of Christians in Communist countries. But there was a multitude on Golgotha who attended the crucifixion of Jesus and the two thieves, who actually heard their cries when nails were driven into their hands and feet, and who must have known that one of those three was the best of men. Who else would have prayed for his torturers? Who else would have cared enough to bring a robber to God, while suffering so intensely himself? Now this Jesus cried out in despair, 'My God, my God, why hast thou forsaken me?'

And the people nodded to one another and said, 'Let be, let us see . . .' It did not even occur to them that they might try to alleviate his suffering. No one brought him water or even spoke a word of compassion. Nothing. Only: 'Let be, let us see whether Elias will come to save him.'

Looking at history we see that apathy has grown over the centuries. Seemingly, it is now reaching a peak as we approach the midnight which the Lord foretold, when a voice will be heard saying, 'Behold, the bridegroom comes, go ye out to meet him' (Matt. 25:6). At that moment even the virginal souls who have waited for him will be fast asleep. The few awake will be those who announce his coming.

Just as midnight is the time when a part of the earth is farthest from the sun, so spiritual midnight is the time when men are at the greatest distance from God. We fast approach this midnight and the awesome events that will accompany it, but midnight does not have the same meaning for children of God as it has for the children of the world. At midnight every firstborn Egyptian boy died, but it was in that same hour that the chosen people were freed.

The Lord said, 'The night comes when no man can work' (John 9:4); but we know that whenever something is declared impossible in the Bible, this does not refer to the faithful, for Jesus declared, 'All things are possible to him that believes' (Mark 9:23). The people of God often accomplish their greatest exploits as midnight approaches. It was midnight when Samson took the gates of the city near Gaza (Judg. 16:3) and when Ruth received the promise from Boaz, 'I will do for you all that you require' (Ruth 3:11). At midnight Paul and Silas won for the Lord the jailer of Philippi (Acts 16:25) and the Psalmist says, 'At midnight I will rise to give thanks unto thee' (Ps. 119:62).

Our mission strove to awaken those who had fallen asleep simply because it was night, as well as those who had been lulled to sleep by the Communists, for part of this insidious sleep in the West is intentionally induced. 'In order to win victory,' wrote Mao-Tse-Tung, 'we must try our best to seal the eyes and ears of the enemy, making him blind and deaf' (*Works*, Vol. II).

Just as we sometimes have to poke someone severely in the ribs to awaken them, so must we also poke the ribs of entire nations. Dostoyevski, the renowned Russian Christian writer, said that when a great nation loses her confidence and no longer believes that she alone possesses the truth that is capable of reviving and redeeming all other nations, then 'she at once becomes a mere ethnographical factor and ceases to be a great nation'. If Westerners really believe that their nations stand for truth, Christianity, and freedom, let their lives exemplify these values and ideals.

In the February 1964 issue of *Reader's Digest*, Nixon wrote, 'The USA's goal must be nothing less than to bring freedom to the Communist world . . . It is high time to put this on the front burner, to make it a top priority objective in every international negotiation.' But when he was elected President four years later, he apparently had forgotten all about this.

Queen Victoria said that Britain's strength was rooted in its fidelity to the Bible. As long as the British believed in the Bible they had an empire. When they lost the Bible, they lost the empire along with it. In the near future they might be in danger of losing even their own isles.

Our mission re-called Westerners to Christ, and gave them an ideal for which to live and die: freedom for our enslaved brethren, liberty for oppressed nations, the spreading of the Gospel to those who are forcibly kept without it.

Holy examples

Nothing sanctifies more than holy examples. Again and again in our lectures we have recounted the heroism of the underground Christians and their children.

A Russian Communist magazine, *Nauka i Religia,* reported that in the village of Burnii a teacher wrote on the blackboard, 'There is no God', and asked the children to read it. One girl raised her hand, stood up and spoke out loud and clear, 'God exists.' According to the article, the children told this teacher the parable of the prodigal son. She then complained that all of her pupils were children of believers – after sixty years of Communist terror all the pupils were Christians, despite the imprisonments and slaughters. This teacher organised an atheist festival but not one child came. The reporter complained that the children spent two to three hours a day in prayer. Even believers in the West would think that was 'too much'. But how much time do Western children spend watching TV? It just shows again how different East and West really are.

Pravda Ukraini reported that its correspondent in the region of Kiev visited the house of a Baptist pastor named Nikolaie Riaboi. The pastor's wife, who had refused to work on the collective farm, met him with the words, 'I and my house serve the Lord.' She went on to tell him that Christ presided over her husband, and that her husband presided over her. She considered that not to be submissive to her husband was a great sin, and so she refused to work on the farm because it belonged to the atheist authorities.

Young believers in the same village told the correspondent, 'We live with the hope that the blessed time will come when, being free from our body of flesh, we will be clothed with a new heavenly body, without any temptations or sins, and then we will be in paradise.' Therefore they avoided the fellowship of unbelievers in their village and refused to marry them.

The same article described a Baptist meeting in the village church of Krivaia. Before the meeting began an atheist agitator was already in the church speaking about the attractions of a worldly life. He delivered his 'sermon' about the new show places and theatres in Kiev, about television, dances on ice, and other such entertainment which believers there consider anathema. To them it is like ingesting poison.

At the edge of Krivaia, there is a house whose windows are covered with black curtains so that no light can be seen from the street. In a small room, men and women kneel on the floor with hands lifted and eyes closed, praying and weeping. It is a meeting of Pentecostals, a sect whose very existence is not recognised or approved by the State. These brethren gather together secretly to pray in one another's homes.

The Underground Church, its persecution, its steadfastness in faith have by now become widely known. When I first spoke about it in the West fifteen years ago, many said I had invented it all.

Sufferings in my mind

In *Tortured for Christ* I wrote that I suffered in the West more than in Communist prisons. Let me explain what I have suffered. During the first years after my release there was the shock of re-entering a world that had so drastically changed. For a time I could not control my nerves. My hands shook almost continually, and I was subject to periods of intense intolerance which caused me great anguish because I seemed unable to control them. The years of prison had left their mark not only on my body but also on my soul and mind.

I wondered why some church leaders could not understand the condition of my mind. They seemed insensitive to the fact that, given the brainwashing and mental anguish to which I had been subjected, I could not possibly have total clarity of mind.

I had lived through fourteen years of Pavlovian treatment. If you condition a dog to salivate in response to a mild electric shock which is the signal for food, and you gradually increase the strength of the current, the dog can bear the stress only up to a certain point. Then he collapses. This type of conditioning is what I endured during those years. We waited for the piece of bread which was given us every three days. The third day would come, but no bread. After hours of expectation, we would knock gently at the door, scarcely daring to remind the warden that it was the day for bread. He would swear at us saying, 'You don't deserve it,' and would beat us instead. How could we not have broken down under such circumstances?

Every animal's nervous system breaks down when it is subjected to periods of prolonged inhibition like waiting under stress. We had been waiting for the Allies to come and release us, as they had promised again and again over the radio. We had been waiting for an amnesty, for a liberalisation of the prison regime. We had been waiting in vain for death to free us. It was not possible to find immediately a rested and peaceful Wurmbrand with whom to enter into easy and harmonious collaboration.

Any clinical psychologist can provoke confusion in a dog's mind by following this procedure: first he accustoms the dog to getting fed when it sees a circle and to being beaten when it sees an ellipse. Then he shows the dog ellipses which are gradually shaped more and more like circles. When the stress becomes too great, the dog can no longer differentiate.

I knew that Christianity was good and Communism was bad. When I came to the West and found Christian pastors flirting with Communism and in fellowship with Communists disguised as friends, while their comrades in other countries openly persecuted the Church, I was incapable of a quiet and rational reaction. I am aware that in some instances I must have shown the ultra-paradoxical reaction shown by Pavlovian dogs after being intentionally confused. The dogs come to react with hatred toward those who show them love and vice versa. When I found myself responding in that way I prayed that those around me would be patient; Jesus still had much work to do with me.

I am conscious of how the mind works and do not rely on it. The Romanian word for 'mind' is also used to mean 'liar'. I rely on the guidance of Jesus, not on the conclusions of my reason alone.

New temptations in the West

I was facing entirely new temptations now. In Hebrews 11:37, being tempted is compared to being stoned, sawn asunder, or slain with the sword. To one with a basically evil nature, temptation is easy to bear. But for the child of God, born again, temptation is a terrible suffering.

I had had no money during those fourteen years in prison. Now the minimal salary I was getting as pastor, which amounted to less than that of an American street sweeper, seemed enormous. To be able to drive around in a car when I had never even owned a bicycle was a tremendous burden. A love for money seemed to develop in me.

I had hardly seen a woman in those fourteen years. Now women and girls surrounded me, many full of love and admiration. I had been a prisoner that anyone who wanted to could slap and spit upon. Now I read articles that said I was 'the most dramatic preacher', that 'since Jesus nobody ever preached with so much love'. I knew that such praise was as false as the unjustified scorn had been in the past. But it pleased my heart and I fell into temptations whose very existence I had forgotten about in prison.

In Numbers 5:12 it is written, 'If any man's wife go aside and commit a trespass against him . . .' Since the Hebrew word for 'go aside' is *tisteh*, the passage could be translated, 'if any man's wife commits folly'. No one sins unless folly has entered him. Fools are acquitted in human courts. Will God not then do the same? In the Greek original of Colossians 2:13 we read, 'He graces our offences.'

Although I have sinned in many respects these past years, I trust in Christ's forgiveness and in the forgiveness of those against whom I have sinned.

I was involved in a fight with a cunning and hateful enemy, and I am continually exposed to the temptation to become like the enemy I fight against. Enemies will transform us into their own image when we fight them back using their own methods.

It was difficult for me to readjust to family life. My wife had grown accustomed to independence, while I, having had to submit to orders in prison without making the slightest objection, had developed a strong desire for self-assertion. Mihai had become alienated from me. He was his mother's son and I had become only a vague remembrance. He had received his faith from me, but had also suffered for bearing my name. Thus his feelings were ambivalent and he had come to wonder: would it not have been wiser for his father to leave the Church and flee rather than expose his son to so much hardship? Now the more my name became known in the world, the more he became known as 'Wurmbrand's son'. But he was definitely a personality in his own right. He quickly achieved three academic degrees while at the same time working for our mission. He wrote a book, and developed amazing administrative capacities which he used for our organisation. He was far from wishing to be a second Richard Wurmbrand.

It was also disorienting to shift from the intense exchanges that occur between men in prison to a simple brotherly relationship with men who had grown up in a world completely foreign to me. Utterly futile personal clashes occurred. My own family, the Harris family and other friends were those who suffered most, but they were also the ones who helped me most during those trying times. I offer here my humble apology for all the suffering which they had to bear because of me.

Becoming famous proved to be a painful burden. I continually felt like a thief. I was preaching and writing about the most beautiful exemplars of mankind, heroes of faith, saints who have died or are still suffering in Communist prisons. Audiences would project that beauty about which I was speaking onto me, and attribute to me personally the halo which surrounds the martyrs.

'Ye shall not steal' (Lev. 19:11) also means not to solicit the good opinion of others by any manner of representation, publicity, flattery or by deceiving others into having a better opinion of a person or his actions than he deserves. We must earn our fellow men's appreciation, not steal it. To steal it had been the sin of Absalom.

But it was in the mission's interest to promote my name, especially in the United States where sophisticated advertising techniques are commonly used to project the leaders of religious organisations to prominent positions in the public eye. No advertising would mean no money coming in, and no money meant no food for Christian martyrs and their families. I hated this advertising, but we had to use it. It was painful for me to see my photograph in newspapers and on posters, or on TV, with any caption other than, 'a miserable sinner saved by grace alone'.

Is there an Underground Church?

The opposition I met within the Church aggravated my state. When *Tortured for Christ* was published in Germany, the head of the Department of Foreign Affairs of the Evangelical Lutheran Church wrote a letter to all its pastors stating that the book was untrue. The Evangelical Lutheran Church wrote an official letter stating that no one in the whole Communist area was in prison for his faith. Voices in other countries agreed. Some church leaders even said I had invented the Underground Church, and asserted that when they themselves had visited Romania, Russia and other places, they had found no trace of it.

This is like the story of the man who, though he had lived his whole life on the sea-shore, fishing, swimming and watching, refused to believe that pearls could be found in the sea. If anyone knew the sea, it was he, and he had never seen one. Indeed, a man must dive to the very bottom and be very lucky in order to find a pearl.

If these same church leaders had travelled to Palestine 2,000 years ago, they would not have met with the Son of God. They would have been on an official visit to the chief priests. Their banquets would not have been attended by Jesus. Quite by accident they might have seen some prisoners being led through the temple yard, none of whom gave any outward sign of being anyone special. The visitors would have said that the report of the Son of God living in Palestine was false.

These church leaders had spoken with many Christians in Communist countries who had told them that no Underground Church existed. Had these same bishops visited Palestine soon after the Lord's ascension to heaven and spoken with the apostles or with Virgin Mary, asking them, 'Is there a Christian Church in Jerusalem?' they would have received the answer, 'No.' The apostles did not know then that their group would later be called the Christian Church. They knew themselves as 'the saints', 'the children of God', 'disciples of Jesus', 'Jews who believe in Jesus as the Messiah', and so on. The first Christians were not called Christians, just as believers in Communist countries today do not know that they constitute what is known abroad as the Underground Church. They only know that they are fulfilling their Christian duty. They gather in homes and forests though it is forbidden, they have secret printing shops, secret Sunday schools, and their leaders are in hiding, but they know of no Underground Church. Western bishops, because of a question of semantics, disputed the existence of the real Church in one third of the world. Since the publication of Solzhenitsyn's books, its existence and persecution is no longer in doubt. But until then we had a hard fight.

We had to say as Savonarola said to Christ, 'You are my superior, you are my priest, you are my bishop, you are my pope,' and pay no attention to the skeptical leaders of some Christian Churches.

Conflicts at World Congresses

We attended the Baptist World Congress in Tokyo with brothers Braun and Neureder of the German mission. Ten thousand delegates were present at the opening meeting, of whom eight thousand were Americans. At the second meeting the hall was nearly empty. Evidently the delegates found it more interesting visiting the international exhibition then running in Osaka. The press paid scarcely any attention to the Congress. The opening speech had stated, 'We stand for baptism by immersion,' a message which was

81

not apt to be popular among atheists, Shintoists and Buddhists.

The Congress began with a parade of the flags of the various countries represented. Although an Israeli delegate was present, the Israeli flag was not displayed because the Soviets do not like Israel and it would have offended the delegations of Baptists from Communists countries. So, although salvation comes from the Jews, out with the Israeli flag. The Czechoslovak flag was also missing. The Soviet invasion of Czechoslovakia was still too fresh in many of our memories and this too would have embarrassed the Soviets. The one flag that was given due honour was the flag of the Soviet Union. Unfortunately this is not the flag of a state but the flag of the Communist International, the flag of world revolution, stained with the blood of countless martyrs. I was the only one to stand up and protest, with the result that I was beaten and thrown out of the meeting. I can assure everyone that this beating was far less severe than the beatings of the Nazis and the Communists had been. The Japanese pastor who hit me was soon rewarded with an invitation to visit Moscow, all expenses paid.

The result of my stay in Japan was the creation of an amazingly strong Japanese Christian Mission to the Communist World, led by brother Yakuwa, in a country where only 1 per cent of the population believes in Christ.

Episodes like those at the Baptist congress in Tokyo did not disturb us much. We knew that the majority of Baptists were wholeheartedly on our side, and that the conflict was with a few isolated leaders. History had taught us that when the Church encounters a new and powerful foe, many Church leaders walk the way of compromise while only a few remain faithful to the end.

My son Mihai and his wife Judith did not fare any better than I. When they attended the World Pentecostal Congress in Dallas, Texas, they found to their surprise that a Soviet delegation appeared and was received with honour. Yet even Soviet publications admit that the Pentecostal religion is forbidden in Russia. Pentecostal Christians are put in psychiatric asylums. Who then were these delegates? Whom did they represent and who had chosen them? Obviously they were sent with the government's approval.

Solzhenitsyn calls such religious leaders the 'ecclesiastic embassy of the Prince of darkness'.

My children protested at the acceptance of these Communist stooges and the persecution of Christians in the Soviet Union. They were manhandled just as I had been in Japan and were thrown out of the Pentecostal Congress while the Communist spies remained.

4: Conflict or compromise

Some Western Church Leaders compromise

In the Catholic Church in the East there are those who compromise with the government, so called peace-priests, who take their name from Pope John XXIII's 'Peace on Earth'. The Czech Communist newspaper *Svobodne Slovo* reported that the purpose of this organisation of priests corresponded exactly with the programme of the Czech Socialist Republic. No comment should be necessary. This Republic is Marxist and Marx taught that all religions and all morals must be abolished.

Polish, Romanian, Lithuanian, and Czech priests make this compromise under the pressure of Communist dictatorship. I know no one who, stopped at gunpoint by a robber and told to give up his wallet, would not hand it over. What is strange, though, is that there should also be such priests in the West, where no gun is pointed at them. The Pope sent Mgr Casaroli, his Minister of Exterior Affairs, to Czechoslovakia to ordain as bishop a priest named Vrana. This priest was a leader of the peace-priests movement and had appeared as a prosecution witness in a trial against faithful Christians. The Communist authorities wanted this man to be a bishop and the Vatican had yielded, forgetting that according to old Church canons such an ordination is invalid: any ordination in which there is state interference is void.

Flattery towards Communists is spread in a large portion of the Catholic camp. *Il Mattino* (Naples) reproduced a document originating from the Jesuit leadership which said that 'the evolution of the Polish situation is positive. Polish Communists have had good results in economic problems.' These Jesuits must have been deaf to what the whole world knew, that proletarians in Danzig and Stettin were shot by the Polish dictatorship because they dared say that a family cannot live on forty dollars a month. The first woman worker who was shot died saying the words, 'Jesus, Mary!' but this did not move any of the Jesuit 'leaders'. I remember meeting Jesuits of another kind in Romanian prisons, priests ready to be tortured and die for their faith.

Let the 'peace-priests' bring God meat offerings made of chaff: the true children of God are on our side and do the finest things for the Lord, as God did the finest thing for us on Good Friday, the day which completed the offering foretold by the Jewish Passover.

Hungarian bishops made a resolution which showed what spirit animated them: 'The principles and practice of justice in Hungary bear the name "socialism".' What name would they give the injustice which tortured Catholics in prison?

The priest Guilio Girardi was one of the experts at Vatican II who determined that, in spite of the request of 600 bishops, the assembly should not condemn Communism as an intrinsically evil doctrine. Later he was expelled from his professorship of theology because he openly declared himself a Marxist Christian.

The wolf in sheep's clothing had been discovered, but too late. One cannot be a Marxist Christian any more than one can be a devilish disciple of Christ. There is no compromise possible between a burning torch and a barrel of gasoline.

Marx was a devil-worshipper connected with a Satanist sect, as I amply demonstrated from his own writings in my book, *Was Karl Marx a Satanist?*

The fashionable Marxist trend among priests and pastors spreads like wildfire. The Assistant Archbishop of Saigon (Vietnam), Franz Xaver Nguyen Van Thuan, and several Protestant leaders were denounced by Marxist priests, nuns and pastors and jailed. To sit in prison for your belief in Christ is not depressing, but it *is* depressing to know that those who denounced you are fellow brethren with whom you once ate sacred bread, and who have since taken the name of 'progressives' in order to please Satanist tyrants.

From all Eastern countries warnings come to the World Council of Churches, to the Vatican, to the Baptist World Alliance, etc, that the church leaders appointed by Communists should not be trusted. Christians ask for open protest against their persecutors instead of diplomacy, but such requests are swept under the rug.

Many leaders of the universal Church do not realise what an abyss separates Christianity from Communism. After all the disclosures about the mass-slaughters that were perpetrated by the Communists, the French Protestant pastor Richard Mollard writes, 'I dare to hope that, because of hastened social and political evolution in the world today, the French Communist Party will evolve . . . towards a true respect for those who do not share its beliefs, and towards an authentic democratic freedom.' This is as wise as hoping for the devil's conversion, or that social evolution will produce crocodiles that do not eat men.

Some of the clergy betray Christianity in the West, others betray it in the East. Protestant leaders live under the same illusion as Catholics.

I once spoke with a Protestant bishop who had been impressed by Hromadka, a Czech professor of theology who was then touring the West praising Communist 'liberties'. The bishop had visited Czechoslovakia himself and had seen these liberties with his own eyes. This had been under Novotny's dictatorship. When Dubcek overthrew him, there was a short-lived attempt to introduce a socialism with a human face in Czechoslovakia. The press became free for a little while. In its 31 May, 1968 issue, the magazine *Cultural Life*, published in Bratislava, wrote that under the old regime, 'the Lutheran church had been crippled in its activity and almost totally incapacitated . . . Only a man chosen by the state could be elected to any church office . . . The church as a whole had been in prison since 1950 . . .' So, the American bishop had visited a Church 'in prison' and had not even noticed that he had seen her behind bars. Innumerable Church leaders in the West continue to suffer from the same blindness.

Other free world Church leaders simply betray the Church. The Protestant Federation of France published a document expressing their sympathy for revolution. They wrote that 'the victory of the truth of the Gospel . . . cannot be accomplished in any way other than by revolutionary fight.' But they have never seen a Communist revolution.

Russian Christians lived through a revolution and learned to hate Communism.

The Russian Orthodox Church of America knew that Pimen's election as Patriarch of the Soviet Union was a farce. He had been nominated by the Communist Party and everyone knew his life story. While Pimen was Bishop of Leningrad he had not protested while half the churches in his diocese were closed. Later, as Bishop of Kolyma, he suspended the heroic priests Eshliman and Yakunin who opposed the subservience of the Moscow Patriarchy to the atheist government. He called Svetlana Stalina a 'Judas Iscariot' when she defected, and in the 2 July, 1967 issue of *Izvestia*, he wrote that religion had never been persecuted in the Soviet Union.

Orthodox Churches in the free world and other Western Churches added prestige to the farce of such patriarchal elections by their support. The American Orthodox Church even asked this spurious church for canonicity.

Cardinal Konig, representing the Pope, remained silent when the new Patriarch, at his enthronment, repeated the patent lie that Ukranian Greek-Catholics had united with the Orthodox of their own accord. In the Vatican Cardinal Konig had met the Ukrainian Cardinal Slipji who had spent eighteen years in Siberia for opposing this forced reunion, which had cost the lives of so many bishops, priests, and thousands of laymen.

Patriarch Pimen's philosophy was simple: when the believers from Neftogorsk asked him to intervene with the authorities who hindered them from opening a church, he replied, 'If the authorities do not agree with the opening of a church, it means that God does not want it to be opened.' It is shameful for a man who is supposed to be an avant-garde fighter for the freedom of religion to make such an unchallengeable statement.

Another example of the duplicity of some church leaders is that of Alexander Karev. This man, after spending many years in Communist prisons for his faith, later became general secretary of the Official Baptist Union of the Soviet Republics. When he died the real Church, the Underground Church, had excommunicated him.

Some people believe we should never say anything negative about someone who is dead. In this case the apostles were wrong to report Judas' betrayal decades after he had hanged himself. And we are all wrong to recite a creed which accuses Pilate, a man who has been dead for two thousand years. A person's wrong actions may continue to exist long after his physical death.

Karev had been a church leader, but in the latter part of his life he was no longer a lover of good. When he died he was working on an article for *Bratskii Vestnik*, the official organ of Communist stooges among the Baptists. In a previous article he called Lenin a 'sociologist humanist', and praised Lenin's books even though they are full of hatred for religion. A church leader should be a lover of good, not of tyranny.

The book *Let History Judge* by the Russian Communist Roy Medvedev (Alfred Knopf, New York, 1971), describes some of the tortures applied to prisoners in the Leninist jails of the Soviet Union. This source is unchallengable and details the methods used by Lenin's followers to force confessions from innocent people, among whom were many Christians. Sons were often killed in front of their mothers to make the mothers confess non-existent crimes. A prisoner who refused to denounce others would be shown a stranger and told that the man would be shot if the prisoner refused to co-operate. If the prisoner, thinking it was a trick, still resisted, the hostage was shot. After a few days a second person was shot before his eyes. To prevent others from being executed the prisoner denounced his friends, who later on were also killed.

I could give numerous other examples.

For many of the church leaders, Savonarola's words hold true: 'Our contemporary prelates and preachers, with very few exceptions, are fit for the destruction of Christian life rather than for its edification and keeping.'

Savonarola also said, 'A voice is crying: "Shout!" and what do you shout? Clergy, clergy, clergy! Because of you, all this storm has got loose. Oh, clergy, you are the principal cause of evil. Because of your lives, there is a storm. I must speak to you! Step forward, you cursed Church! In lasciviousness you have become a shameless whore. Everybody knows your sin. You have become a devil, you have debased yourself to an animal, a horrible monster. After all your shameful deeds, captivity will be your fate. Woe to your leaders! Woe to the others! Woe to all! Nothing but suffering stands before you!'

We should not forget that Savonarola himself was a priest.

Savonarola's words were not polite or polished, nor are mine. We have no commandment to be nice. Our duty is to be faithful to the Lord. Will we be heeded? We do not care. Christ gave his life for us without the guarantee that we would return his love. Out of love for the flock led astray and for the leaders who endanger their souls, we too must cry, 'Clergy, clergy, clergy!'

Having to utter such a cry was another great suffering for me.

Suffering the sting of objectivity

There are those who love the persecuted Church and those who oppose it. In a third category are those who commit the sin of being 'objective'.

A criminal named Tsirekidze was detained in the Tbilisi jail (Soviet Union). In a petition addressed to the authorities, he described being used by Communist police officers to obtain false, self-incriminating statements from fellow prisoners by means of torture and provocation. He acknowledges having personally beaten other prisoners to death and having commited homosexual abuses in compliance with orders he received. He and other criminals employed by the police were rewarded with alcohol, drugs and prostitutes.

To gain their fellow-prisoners' confidence, they posed as rebels, going to the extent of slitting their wrists and then being rescued at the last moment. They would be placed in a punishment cell where they would go hungry, sleep on the cold, damp concrete, and make friends with their future victims by suffering with them. Then they would begin torturing them. To be tortured by those you consider friends is a maddening pain.

Such crimes are common practice in Communist prisons. I experienced them myself in the Romanian jails.

One of the most interesting features of Tsirekidze's confession is the use of the word 'object' for the man assigned to be tortured. For example: 'The agent Agdgomelashvili beat bloodily the object Iskanderashvili . . . Agent Uspulian beat the object Kuhianidze . . . There were beatings in all the cells, and the jail was filled with the screams and cries of the objects.'

'Object' – this is how prisoners, among them our Christian brethren, are designated by the Communist police. It is the exact fulfillment of Lenin's thoughts: 'You cannot fry eggs without breaking the shells. You cannot cut wood without making chips fly. So you cannot make revolution without killing men.' Lenin did not know the difference between eggshells, wood and human suffering. To him his adversaries were objects.

'Objectivity' in human affairs, in conflicts between nations, races, parties, denominations, reduces men to objects of research and experiment.

Some former Soviet prisoners who appeared on a German television series estimated the number of political prisoners presently detained in the Soviet Union at 1,200,000. Others claim there were only 100 Christians in jail. Which is the correct figure? Neither. Suffering men are not figures; they are not objects, they are *me*.

The Lord Jesus asked the future apostle Paul, 'Saul, Saul, why persecutest thou *me*?' (Acts 9:4). Saul of Tarsus could have truthfully answered, 'I do not persecute *you*; I persecute only your disciples.' But Jesus does not make any distinction between himself and a disciple. His disciples are himself. His suffering brothers and sisters not objects of his thoughts, of his cares, of his love – they are himself; they are and will always be subjects.

If imprisoned Christians were mere objects, it would make no difference whether there were hundreds of thousands or only a few. But our suffering brethren are not objects; they are 'partakers of the divine nature' (2 Pet. 1:4). The Church is Jesus' body (Col. 1:18). He is in prison even if only a single brother suffers there. He is me, because 'not I live, but Christ' (Gal. 2:20). Christ, who identifies himself with the sufferer; he is my real 'I'. For myself I am always subject, not object. 'Wurmbrand totally rejects scholarly objectivity', was the big headline in *Reformatorisch Dagbladet* (Holland). So be it.

Objectivity when applied to human beings is wrong. We must passionately stay on the side of truth and love and remain blind and deaf to our enemies' arguments. The Church of Christ is right. Its oppressors and traitors, those who compromise with the tyrants, are wrong and despicable. There can be no in-between. God himself said, 'I will put enmity between the seed of the woman [the Saviour] and the seed of the serpent' (Gen. 3:15). Enmity – not objective research, compromise and peaceful co-existence.

This applies to Communist persecution of Christians, to political and private life – to all relationships between groups of men. Righteousness must triumph.

Our mission fulfills the simple duty of every Christian to be anti-Communist. A leader of a Californian-based Christian organisation declared, 'I would not wish to give the impression that we are anti-Soviet, or anti-Russian, or even anti-Communist.' Anyone who is not anti-Communist is not Christian, just as anyone who is not anti-Satan is not Christian. Marxism is satanic, as I have shown in my book *Was Karl Marx a Satanist?* The Communist doctrine cannot be Christianised any more than the devil's legions can be evangelised. Our mission rejects any objectivity in this matter and advises you, when you stand for a righteous cause, to reject 'objectivity' too.

There are Christians in prison for their faith in the Soviet Union. Whether they are two or two million makes no difference to us, except for practical purposes in conveying your contributions to their families. Their suffering is devastating to our lives because they and we and Christ are all one. We see no distinction. They are our own life.

Prisoners are no longer simply shot as in the past. They are put to slave labour. A Russian Orthodox priest, driven to despair, wrote from the concentration camp: 'I wanted to force martyrdom on myself. I have tempted God, but in his unfathomable plan he has refused me. There is no martyrdom in the camp, at least not the martyrdom suffered by the great saints of our church. Here there is only work for the Bolshevik system in which man is gradually consumed like a candle which burns down until it is extinguished. Through martyrdom, the man of faith can conquer Satan, and if his sacrifice is pleasing to God, he will enter into the ranks of saints. But by labour, Satan can conquer the man of faith, enslave him, make use of him, exploit him to the bitter end for his own satanic aims. This knowledge is the most terrible temptation that Satan has so far set before me. Pray for me, that this satanic despair will leave me.'

This is, 'objectively' speaking, the despair of a single man. But it torments our hearts as though millions of sufferers for Christ were likewise being tempted into unbelief under the pressure of Communist torture. We wholeheartedly hate this system. We find no excuse for it. Our mission has no time for historical explanation. Our present aim is to help the persecuted Church with Bibles, Christian literature, broadcasts, and relief for the families of prisoners. Our ultimate goal is that Russia and all the other Communist countries be freed from Satan's rule. Because we do not aim at 'objectivity' but at victory, we publish statements that stir up passion in this fight. This principle applies to all Christian work and warfare. It applies to all involvement in a righteous cause.

In practice there is no difference between the sting of objectivity and the persecution of an outspoken enemy. The pain one suffers is the same.

Various pains

I also suffered for being identified with what is commonly called the anti-Communists. Though hating Communism, I did not feel like an 'anti-Communist'.

Christ's commandment 'Love your enemies' is a concession to our weakness. Normally a Christian should have no enemies. A Christian is not inimical towards the Communists. He is an anti-Communist; what he hates is the doctrine and its crimes against mankind. A Christian simply cannot be a foe. He is an understanding friend. His understanding encompasses not only the sick but also the sickness. Charity believes all things (1 Cor. 13:17), it enables men to realise that in certain circumstances Communism is the only ideological outcome possible.

While loving, Christians must also fight certain men and institutions. This fight is waged on many fronts. Every man is responsible only for his own sector of the battle.

I too had to concentrate on one sector of the Christian fight. But this threatened to prevent me from appreciating the whole gamut of human experience. I was alarmed to observe in myself a certain disinterest in any suffering other than that in the Communist camp, while our duty is to be united with all men of good will who, in any department of life, are doing their best to further the Kingdom.

The Communists could not see that I loved them, just as the Pharisees did not know that Jesus loved them. It was only normal that the Reds should react overtly as well as covertly. Their attacks often gave me great pain.

The Soviet press published numerous articles against my counter-revolutionist, Fascist activity (for them any opponent is a Fascist), asserting in addition that my wife and I were running a bordello and nine night-clubs. The Bulgarian Communist press also attacked us. Radio Tirana was upset when Gospels we had launched from a ship were found on their shores. The leftist press of the West joined in and even some Christian publications published articles against the mission and against me.

The writing on the wall

I am seated with Christ in heavenly places, and from there I look at those who find fault with me as I would look at people who would spit at heaven. Spittle soils neither heaven nor those seated there – but comes back to defile the person who spat it out.

As a child of God I cannot be hurt. Every misery that others would inflict on me returns to the sender. I belong to the privileged group of those who are beloved, without any merit on their part, just as we love our children.

I desire one thing: Christ's triumph in the Communist world. Kierkegaard wrote, 'Purity of heart consists in willing one thing.' Although it is not an exhaustive definition, we have purity of heart in this sense. And therefore we see God on our side.

Having this assurance, I will make one last comment about the opposition I encountered from church leaders.

Once, as King Belshazzar of Babylon was revelling with his lords and women, words written in Aramaic appeared on the wall. The king immediately summoned his counsellors to read it and explain the significance of such an unusual event. None of the counsellors knew what to say. Belshazzar called Daniel and complained to him, 'The wise men, the astrologers, have been brought in before me, that they should read this writing, and make known unto me the interpretation thereof: but they could not show the interpretation of the thing' (Dan. 5:15).

The writing was in Aramaic, the language spoken by the Jews, who made up an important national minority in the Babylonian empire – a minority which had given the country a prime minister and other dignitaries. But none of the wise men of Babylon had made any effort to learn the language, religion or mental outlook of this minority.

Babylon's enemies, the Medes and Persians, were already at the city gates. That night King Belshazzar was slain and the city fell into enemy hands. Babylon's wise men had no wisdom. They did not know the imminence of the danger and had not been able to warn the king.

The tragic ignorance of the wise men is repeated today. Important leaders of the universal Church are wise enough to secure for themselves the benefits and fame of leadership, but they do not know what is happening within the people they are meant to lead towards Christ, nor do they comprehend the destructive forces which threaten the Church. They do not recognise the imminent danger of Communism to Christianity.

Ignorance reigns, not only about what is happening in the Communist world, but also about what is happening in the free world.

The warning to King Belshazzar had been written by a hand on the wall. The warning to the West is written with blood, but our wise men cannot read it.

John F. Kennedy was killed by Moscow-trained Lee Harvey Oswald. Robert F. Kennedy was killed by Sirhan Sirhan, who had written these words in his notebook, 'Communism is the best social system'. The disturbances at major universities across the world have been aroused by a small core of professional leftist militants bent on violence. Acts of terror occur everywhere. Strikes incited by the Communists destroy the economy of whole nations. But most of the wise men in Western churches cannot read this warning. Ask your church leaders whether they have studied Marxism and the philosophy of the new left. Ask them also whether this subject is offered in any seminary or Bible school. You will find that most of them know Marxism as little as the wise men of Babylon knew the Aramaic language. Therefore they cannot read the warning written in blood. Therefore they do not take adequate measures to win Communists and those they influence for Christ.

I do not intend to boast, but when 60,000 leftists marched on the Pentagon on 21 October, 1967, I was the only clergyman present to speak to them about Christ. I took a cherry picker, and hoisted thirty feet above the marchers, preached to the 60,000 immortal souls led astray by the Communists. The wise men of Washington were not there.

After a debate with leftist Professor Wilkinson at San Fernando Valley College, more than twenty radical students openly declared that they had accepted Christ. One of them said, 'Yesterday I had my last kick with LSD. My next kick will be with Jesus.'

When I visited Quezon City, capital of the Philippines, I found the majority of students were Catholics. A few were Evangelical. There were only a handful of Communists, but they dominated. The walls were covered with pictures and sayings of Lenin and Mao. Nowhere was there an image of Jesus or a Bible verse. At the end of my meeting, I tore down a large poster of Lenin as Gideon had overthrown the image of the false god Baal. When some Communists threatened to beat me, the Christian students took my defense. I was told that the debate about what I had done lasted many weeks after that. New courage had entered the hearts of those who belonged to God.

Communist youth can be criticised or approved, arrested or shot; but they can also be won for Christ. This is the goal towards which our mission is working.

The many who love us

In Genesis 35:22, we read that Reuben lay with Bilhah, his father's concubine, and Israel heard it. The word 'it' is added by the translator. In the Hebrew text, the ancient editors, the Massoretes, indicated here 'a pause in the middle of the verse'. In the scrolls of the Law in every synagogue there is a blank space in the text at this place to indicate that the story of an evil must not be completely told. The Bible often abruptly drops a subject when the theme is distasteful.

Why should I report all the evil that has been claimed against us? The fact that we had enemies also served to our credit. A film the Soviets made against us and their vituperations in the press proved that we had hit them hard. A letter criticising me written by a Baptist mission in America ended with the assurance that 'Wurmbrand's Bibles arrive behind the Iron Curtain.'

On the other hand, the attacks against us have been more than counter-balanced by the appreciative words we have received from Christians as well as non-Christians throughout the world.

Israelis generally do not like Hebrew-Christians, and I am the only such Christian praised in the editorial of the *Jerusalem Post*. I was the only Protestant pastor whose book, *In God's Underground*, was praised in four columns in *Osservatore Romano*, the Vatican's publication.

But now about the many brothers and sisters who express their love towards our mission.

Once, when I was at the Los Angeles airport, I approached a sailor at the newsstand and asked him if he was a believer. He answered, 'What a question! I have been one for about six weeks! What about you?'

'But don't you see my collar?' I replied. 'I am a pastor.'

The sailor did not allow himself to be deflected. 'I did not ask you how you earn your living. I asked you if you believed in Jesus Christ.'

'For almost forty years,' I said.

He went on investigating. 'What kind of a Christian are you?'

'A Lutheran.'

'I don't care about that. I want to know if you are a Christian who helps his brethren who suffer in Communist prisons.'

'Why are you asking me this?'

The sailor grew animated. 'You better read a book. I

don't remember the name of the guy who wrote it, – a complicated name – but the title is *Tortured for Christ*. Read the book. You will weep, and pray, and help. Jesus said, "I was in prison and you visited me." If you forget about your brethren in jail, you are not the right type of Christian.'

'I know the guy who wrote the book,' I said. 'In fact his wife and son happen to be at the airport right now.'

The sailor asked to be introduced, and was so happy to meet the family of 'the guy' that he completely forgot about me. 'For the joy of having met you folks I will give a hundred dollars for your mission.' He was only a cook in the navy. Then, unexpectedly, my son addressed me as 'Father'. The man turned to me, 'Then *you* are the guy!' he exclaimed embracing me. 'What a joy! I will give you another forty dollars.'

Believers sometimes travelled thousands of miles to hear about their brethren in Russia, China or Romania. When I preached in Helsinki, they came from Lapland, the extreme north of Finland. When I preached in Wisconsin, a newspaper owner came from Alaska. He had first heard about us from an Eskimo who had been instrumental in his conversion and had aroused in him a living interest in the Underground Church by giving him one of my books to read.

One night we arrived very late at a Christian hotel in South Africa. We had had trouble with the car. The night clerk showed us to our room and added, 'The room next door is free, so you may use it too if you would like.' When I pushed open the door to the adjoining room, a dresser with a mirror fell to the ground. Frightened, a lady in a nightgown jumped from her bed saying, 'Who are you, sir, and what are you doing in my room at this time of night?' 'I am Richard Wurmbrand,' I said, 'and I was told this room was vacant.' Then she shook my hand happily, 'What a surprise. I have read all about you. Happy to meet you.' She forgot completely about the embarrassing circumstances of our meeting, and the next morning she made a generous contribution to our mission.

Dagen, the Pentecostal Daily of Sweden, reported: 'Wurmbrand cries loud, and although not everything he says is suitable for living-room discussions, we forgive him, because within a few years he has managed to direct our

attention to frightful injustices about which it is not oppor-
tune to speak in all Christian circles.'

Norra Skane, another Swedish newspaper, commented:
'Richard Wurmbrand, tortured in Communist prisons,
shows in his book, *Wurmbrand Letters,* that the political
system, idolised as a god, is a monster which can only be
tamed by the bonds of our conscience with Jesus, and which
has been bridled throughout the centuries by the blood of
the martyrs . . . Wurmbrand's book ought to be compul-
sory reading in political science courses in schools.'

We can thank God. Our mission has won millions of
friends for the Underground Church. Millions in a world
with a population of four billion, out of which approximately one quarter are called Christian.

We do not fool ourselves. The majority of Christians,
church leaders and laymen alike, have remained apathetic
to our appeal. They remained unmoved even at the loud
voice of Solzhenitsyn. Even Jesus himself was not received
by his own people.

Apathy comes from our hearts. Every man has within
himself a defense mechanism against things which disturb
him. Whenever we get bad news, the first reaction is, 'Oh,
no, it can't be possible,' even though it can. The idea that
hundreds of millions of innocents are suffering atrocities,
and that the Communist regime could become victorious in
the free world is too terrible to accept. The stain of original
sin on the human character makes us reluctant to accept the
whole message of the cross, of the cross of Golgotha, and of
the cross borne today by the believers in Communist countries.

On our side are the children of God, those whose hearts
are open for His message. We will continue to strive
together to make Jesus king of all. We hope that our wish
will one day be fulfilled. But how this will come about, none
of us can know.

Every peasant works the field he has. A stony field has
been allotted to us. We have to spread our Lord's message
to a world which has forgotten about almost half of
mankind who suffer under Communism.

5: By all means

The real and the fake Underground Church

Everywhere we have met large missionary organisations which call themselves 'world-wide', or publicise 'world-wide' programmes. When we have inquired, we have found that the Communist world was not included.

Our mission fills this gap.

We now publish monthly newsletters in eighty-eight languages. I have had twelve books published in fifteen years. My wife and son have had books published, and a lot of the books have been translated into many languages. My daughter-in-law, too, has recently published a book – in fact, the only one in our family who has not yet written a book is my grand-daughter. She will have to be excused. She is only nine.

We have made contact with underground churches of various confessions in many countries. This was always very hazardous, and demanded much skill, for there is a real Underground Church and a fake one organised by the Communists themselves. The Soviets organise fake political dissenters, protesting writers, and religious secret activities – all of them as noisy as possible. Since their long-range goal is to lull the West to sleep, they want the free world to think: 'No danger from the Soviet side – they have too much dissatisfaction within their own country. When they cannot even crush their own opposition, surely they have no time to think of attacking us.'

The fake underground movement is also used for internal purposes. Kravchenko, a renowned defector from the Soviet Union who wrote *I Chose Liberty*, a book which was quite popular at one time, mentioned having seen a secret printing press in Kemerovo. Incitement to rebellion and leaflets against Stalin were printed there, but the operation was really organised by the Secret Police. The printers were men whose silence could be counted on, prisoners about to be executed or sentenced to life imprisonment. Printing took place at night, supervised by Communist officers. These leaflets served as *corpus delicti* in many trials against innocent persons. The accused all pleaded guilty.

Some well-intentioned organisations in the West are eager to help the persecuted Christians in Communist countries. But what would you say about someone who practices medicine without first having studied it, and justifies himself by saying, 'I do it out of charity'?

Underground work is a science and an art which presupposes years of theoretical and practical study, plus an innate talent.

Couriers who pass the Communist borders often meet men on the other side who give the impression of being exquisite Christians, eager to accept the Bibles or literature smuggled in. They speak intelligently about the Bible, and they know how to pray according to circumstances, in the Orthodox, Catholic, Baptist, or Pentecostal manner. Some of them can even prove that they have suffered for the Lord. The couriers depart, happy that they have found the right contact with the Underground Church, when in fact they have met officers of the Secret Police who have either studied theology extensively, or were real Christians who have broken down under torture and were now ready to play a double role.

Divomlikov in *The Traitor* described the story of a Soviet Orthodox bishop. Formerly a Secret Police agent who had killed priests during the war, he later received the assignment to become a priest, and an especially holy one in whom people would have confidence and confess what they would not tell others. When he was in the seminary he was very strict in prayer, fasting and leading a pure life. When Communists came to confiscate some valuable ikons from the seminary, he was the only one to try to defend the holy images. His comrades beat him and kicked his teeth out. When he became a priest he organised secret Sunday schools and dared to preach what others did not. Even high Communist officials had confidence in him and confessed to him that they were believers. He denounced them all. Some were shot.

In the Orthodox church a married priest cannot become a bishop, so, with some comrades, he staged a deadly car accident for his wife who was a true Christian and had not the slightest suspicion about her husband's real identity. Then he was ordained bishop. As the choir was singing, 'Ye host of martyrs, pray that he might be a worthy bishop,' he amused himself by imagining how the crowned martyrs would pray for him. He had helped them to become martyrs.

In the end, however, the years of prayer and Bible study that he spent preparing for his double role unexpectedly brought him to conversion.

I do not know the author personally, but I have received a similar written confession from a Russian Orthodox leader who was delegated by the Soviets to the World Council of Churches. A Romanian Orthodox priest who had had a hand in my arrest and condemnation disclosed his double role as servant of God and Communist agent when sent to a Christian congress in Upsala. When he was dying, he confessed his sin, and requested that I be asked to forgive him.

In Gallehue's book, *The Jesuit*, mention is made of a Vatican mission to organise a secret Catholic church in Russia when Pius XII was Pope. One of the members of this mission was an agent of the Communist Police and hundreds of Catholics were imprisoned or killed because of him.

For obvious reasons I cannot give names or tell of all the circumstances, but we have the written confession of one of the leaders of the official Orthodox church in a Communist country, a man highly appreciated by the World Council of Churches and the Vatican. He wrote: 'We are rascals and traitors, we denounced, we sold brothers and parents, we are outlaws. Forgive us if you can. We wanted to survive . . . We did not find the formula to live without soiling ourselves. Our only choice was between death and dirt . . . We have suffered perhaps more than the prisoners . . . They will return with the halo of martyrs. We will remain forever with bowed heads, infamous traitors that we are. To live, we took the risk of baseness, and we have to bear that stigma until somebody forgives us . . . We did not know how to harmonise our desire to live with the necessity of remaining pure. We did not say "pure at any price". The price of honesty was too high for us. We chose our own liberty at the price of depriving others of theirs. We realise now that what is important is not to live, but to live morally.'

Such men, branded by their own consciences, are nonetheless accepted in the West as true church leaders rather than as men needing to repent and be saved.

A month before the Ukrainian Bishop Welychkowsky was arrested, a Soviet agent, posing as a French tourist acting on behalf of high church authorities in the West, had asked the bishop for information about the Church's secret activities in the Ukraine to take back to Europe. The agent produced forged accreditation and the bishop gave him written information. This incident explains why so many sincere Western Christians and church leaders come back from Communist countries saying, 'We heard nothing about an Underground Church.' The Church has learned not to disclose its secrets to foreigners.

The Communists are masters of deceit. Bronch-Buievich, one of the founders of the Russian Bolshevik Party, discloses in his books how the revolutionists began to infiltrate the churches even in Czarist times, from the very foundation of the Party.

A world-renowned European pastor was asked by Mr Murgu, counsellor of a Romanian embassy, to publicly attack me in exchange for the freedom to preach in Romania. The embassy promised to provide him with material for the attack. What documents cannot be forged by Communists? The pastor refused. Later on, when this pastor visited Romania he was detained by the police and asked again to infiltrate our organisation. When he again refused, the Communists arrested brethren with whom he had been in friendly contact to blackmail him.

Infiltrators and kinesics

We had no doubts that the Communists would send infiltrators into our ranks to find out our secrets. We received them courteously, not revealing that we knew their assignment. Often we got their secrets instead.

The principle of discovering spies within an underground organisation is easy to grasp. Man is not intended to be a traitor, nor a criminal. When he commits wrong actions there is always a conflict of conscience in him which causes him to make errors. This is why criminals leave fingerprints or personal objects on the scene of the crime. No perfect criminal exists.

Traitors and infiltrators also have divided hearts. Every traitor loudly proclaims being one, not through his speech, but through body language (the subject of a new branch of psychology called Kinesics). We must learn to interpret this.

Notice how many of the Lord's gestures are reported in the Gospel; stretching out his hand, lifting his eyes, touching. The body speaks. Sign language was man's first means of communication and words were only supplementary. Body language has deep facets in man and speaks more eloquently than words.

When a person sees something exciting the pupils of the eye become enlarged. A male's pupil doubles its size when he sees a female nude. The pupils of an underground worker in a Communist country will undoubtedly expand when he sees a Bible.

A thief can rarely look anyone straight in the face. If he does master himself enough to do so, his eyes will continue to speak by over-compensating. His gaze will be too strong, as if he were saying, 'See, I can look at you.'

I once watched a man who probably was an infiltrator walking down a street. He played the role of a sailor who had defected to Canada and was now allegedly converted after a history of brutality towards Christians. He did not walk like a man burdened by the memory of past sins however. It was the proud walk of a youngster who knew he was successfully fulfilling a risky assignment. The Bible says that Ahab repented and walked softly (1 Kgs. 21:27).

I know a man who is deeply involved in Bible smuggling. When he shakes hands, he pushes you away from him as if to warn you to be on guard. With this gesture he expresses his real sentiments: 'Beware of me. The police may be watching. I cannot escape my role, but you should be careful.'

Disbelief causes a specific lift of the eyebrow which can be observed when the Gospel truth is proclaimed to one who is only pretending to be a disciple. Indifference produces a shrugging of the shoulder, noticeable in an informer during a sermon which would impassion a true believer.

People turn up the corners of their mouths when they are happy and turn them down when discontent. But believers and an informer in their midst do not take pleasure in the same things. Careful observation will reveal the difference.

A police officer masquerading as a Christian would enter a room without knocking or immediately after knocking, before getting permission. This is a habit he has acquired in his profession and will reveal him as an impostor.

Dogs will not befriend traitors.

Dishonest men cannot bear powerful music such as Beethoven and will walk out when it is played, because it stirs up the depths of the heart.

Observation of body-speech is common sense for people in all walks of life. Understanding of this science can make relationships more harmonious. A man who says he loves a girl while shaking his head side to side contradicts his claim, unless he is an Indian. Among Indians, shaking the head is a sign of approval.

Some Christians ask in despair, 'How can you work in Communist countries when there are so many informers?' The answer is, 'Learn kinesics.' Much experience is required however to thoroughly understand the language of the body. A facial tick can speak volumes.

Another principle in underground work is always to presume that everyone, without exception, denounces and denounces and denounces again. No member of the Underground Church can have complete confidence in his brother. Everyone must be considered a potential traitor. The children and wives of martyrs are no exceptions, nor are men who have spent many years in prison. An example is the afore-mentioned Karev who was excommunicated from the Church but who had formerly been in prison for Christ.

So we have learned to distinguish the fake Underground Church from the real one.

With appropriate precaution, we have succeeded in

smuggling great quantities of Bibles, Bible portions and other Christian literature into Communist countries.

But the problem of competence in this field has remained a burning one. Not every worker in the Lord's field is a good one. There are also evil workers. This is true in all spheres of church activity, but specially in our domain.

Underground church and mission work in Communist countries is not for amateurs, but only for highly dedicated and well trained ones. It presupposes some knowledge of foreign languages, Marxism, Communist police methods and rules of secrecy. The offices and cars of missions like ours can be bugged; telephones can be tapped. The staff must be screened, the offices examined, sensitive papers must be locked away.

A castastrophic lack of caution exists in some missions working in Communist lands. No anti-Communist organisation will be overlooked by Communist infiltrators.

Colson tells in his book, *Born Again,* how despairingly huge the leakage of secret papers from the Pentagon and the White House was. It is even greater from incompetent missions working in Communist countries. As a result, our Soviet brethren are imprisoned.

Jeremiah wrote, 'Cursed be he that does the work of the Lord' (48:10), but does not do it correctly. We had to be as harsh as the prophet. We had to take a public stand against organisations with an aim similar to ours who do the work irresponsibly or deceitfully.

Just as Paul could not avoid a public quarrel with Peter, Barnabas and Mark, we could not be spared the ordeal of conflict with our brethren. We knew our own intentions were correct. Jesus Himself had to quarrel. In the struggle for the triumph of love, sometimes a lover's quarrel erupts.

A stream of Christian literature enters Communist countries

Leningradskaia Pravda wrote about 'a stream of religious literature and leaflets directed towards our country'.

A stream, no less, in their own words.

Out of the hearts of those who believe in Jesus flow rivers of living water, not some small rivulet.

The Russians say the literature is brought by Christians

who come disguised as tourists and who, taking all risks upon themselves, spread it in the official churches, and secretly, or sometimes openly, on the street.

Sovietskaia Bielorussia described how the imprisoned Grikin sent a warning to Christians who are free 'to hide the exchange of letters and literature of foreign origin'.

Voprosi Filosofii, in enumerating the causes of the persistence of religious prejudices, lists the 'distribution of literature, some printed, some written by hand, which comes partly from abroad'.

At a trial of Soviet writers, Galanskov was accused of having met a foreigner in Troitska Sergeivska monastery who introduced herself as Nadia, a very faithful Christian. 'Nadia brought Galanskov religious material from abroad.'

Who can contradict these facts acknowledged by the Soviet press?

Our underground methods work. The Word of God arrives behind the Iron Curtain.

Komsomolskaia Pravda published an article in which the Communist Korobkov expressed amazement that the renowned engineer and poet Valentin had secretly been a baptised believer and had had his son baptised also. Valentin died at twenty-nine. When Korobkov entered the room of his Christian acquaintance, he found everything untouched. Valentin's Gospel lay open with a bookmark at the passage: 'Come unto me, all ye that labour and are heavy laden, and I will give you rest.' The Christian engineer had found rest because organisations like ours smuggle Bibles to these hungry souls.

In a letter received from another Communist country a believer wrote: 'I inform you that yesterday we received your parcel with very dear gifts; hymnals in our language. Many hearty thanks to you from our family and from the church. This is an irreplaceable thing nowadays. For, as you know, there is no new material in our churches, and the old stock is all gone. At present we are copying the songs by hand. We copy the words only, not the music, therefore the songs are sung differently. But now this dear book will give us many things for use in our homes and in the church. For this kind of work we express to you our deepest gratitude.'

A courier writes, 'I had Bibles, New Testaments and so

on hidden in with the clothing. At the border my suitcase containing the most literature was searched very closely, but Christ must have shut the guards eyes for they did not find anything. The bottom of the suitcase was covered with Bibles with just a paper over them, but they did not see them.'

The Moscow magazine *Agitator* reports: 'They bombard our country with books having anti-Soviet content. Sometimes they throw bottles with literature into the sea. They count on the fact that the currents will bring them to the shores of Socialist countries. There were cases when the first and the fourth pages of Soviet newspapers were copied exactly in the West and on the second and third were printed articles and notes with anti-Soviet content. Such newspapers were sent to the USSR under the form of "returns" from Capitalist countries, the person "being unknown at the address". Our foes put their material also in the covers of magazines and books published abroad by leftist organisations. The enemies of Socialism are shrewd and skillful.'

In order to make very clear what kind of material this anti-Soviet literature is, the *Agitator* recounts the results of such activities.

'Lastly, an activation of different religious sects, which are fanatical and do not fulfill the Soviet laws, has been observed. The members of the sect of Evangelical Baptist Christians teach the refusal of participation in social life, the trespassing against the law regarding religious cults. They strive to impart to children their religious views and morals, which are foreign to Soviet men.'

The Communists are furious about the Christian literature smuggled into their countries. Through our efforts, their sailors obtain it, and even if they are not the least interested in religion, they take it. On the black market in the Soviet Union they can get ten to fifteen pounds for a Bible. So much is the Word of God sought and valued there.

In his book *Religion in The Modern Ideological Struggle*, A. Belov describes the head of the Moscow customs office brooding over dozens of books, brochures and leaflets which have been found on tourists, or enclosed in letters to Soviet citizens whose addresses we supply. Materials are sometimes hidden in cases with imported goods. Diplomats (by the way, sometimes Communist diplomats), guides to foreign exhibits, and others help carry in this literature.

When we read Belov's account, in which every word is carefully weighed, we rejoiced to find out that the director of the Moscow customs office has only dozens of such books. Hundreds of thousands enter. From hundreds of thousands they found dozens. That is all right with us. We consider that with these we have paid our customs duties.

The Communist newspaper *Svet Prace* published the complaint of a high customs official in Czechoslovakia that such streams of religious literature enter his country that the offices are not capable of handling it. 'Foreign countries suddenly show an unusual interest in the salvation of souls of Czech and Slovac men, but in reality they work at an ideological diversion.

'The customs officers must fight against this smuggling of religious literature without compromise, exactly as they fight the smuggling of gold coins, or works of art.' (One of the religious leaders of Great Britain compared the smuggling of Bibles with the smuggling of whisky. This religious leader seems to have the same spirit as the Communists.)

The article reports that on the bus line from Vienna to Prague and Karlsbad, 39 religious books were confiscated. At the Bavarian frontier, 36 Bibles and 437 religious books were confiscated from one team of smugglers and, from a Swedish team, 316 copies of the New Testament and dozens of other religious books were taken.

The article finishes with the words, 'These tourists should learn that for them, at the frontier of Czechoslovakia, the signal is red.'

We do not limit ourselves to smuggling. We have also helped establish printing presses within Communist countries – some sophisticated and some primitive. But the Underground Church cannot print enough for her needs, so some literature has to be smuggled in.

All ways and means are good. The Soviets import wheat from the USA and Canada. One Christian at a grain elevator can see that the shipment contains two kinds of food: for both body and soul. The Soviets and other Communist countries buy machines from the West. They don't always work satisfactorily. How should they when they are stuffed with Scriptures? The Soviets and their European satellite countries have over 6 million tourists a year. Who can check the tyres of every car? Who can check all cars to be sure that they don't have a double floor with Gospels hidden in between? Sometimes the customs officers check that there is no double floor. Finding none, they apologise and allow the car to pass. The Gospels were in the double roof of the car. Among 6 million tourists there are many pregnant women. Some of them have in their 'womb' not an infant but Gospels.

We have studied the ocean currents to enable us to drop Christian booklets in the sea for the tide to carry to Chinese, Russian, Albanian, and Cuban shores. They are wrapped in plastic bags which contain a straw to make them float and a stick of chewing gum to entice children to pick them up.

But are the smuggled Bibles not confiscated? Usually not, but some surely are. However, the confiscated material also reaches the public. A Communist Sokolov was arrested in Moscow. He was a worker in the department which makes sure that no forbidden religious literature enters the country. He confiscated a lot of it. He had a net of secret booksalesmen who made it available to those who thirsted for the Word of God.

Is it righteous to smuggle Bibles?

God did not stop at the human level of morals when our salvation was at stake. It is not praiseworthy for a father to send his innocent son to death. It is even less commendable for him to stand by and see him betrayed, flogged, and crucified when he has the power to save him. But our heavenly Father not only allowed his son to die: 'It pleased the Lord to bruise him' (Isa. 53:10). What is highly immoral according to common standards becomes an act of love if it results in the salvation of men.

If God gave his Son to die for this purpose, we also feel justified in sidestepping some of the norms of ordinary Christian behaviour. We use original methods to smuggle Bibles in order that God's creatures in Communist lands might enter God's heaven.

We smuggle the Word of God to those who hunger for it. Some say that to do so is immoral. We consider it immoral to leave souls without the Word of God. Would you consider it immoral to help starving children because a government forbids foreign aid? Is not food for the soul as important as food for the body?

But is it right to smuggle and not say the plain truth?

Jews answer questions with another question. This I will do, too. Is it right to apply some yardstick of morality to the means of spreading the Word of God? If we apply a yardstick, with what yardstick will we measure the yardstick according to which we consider some actions right and some wrong?

I wonder why the ethical problem of one's obligation to tell the truth is restricted to the field of providing Communist countries with Bibles.

Can a Christian in a free country belong to the police or the intelligence service? If so, can he accept an assignment as an undercover agent in a group of terrorists, in a spy ring, or in an organisation of drug pushers? If so, must he tell the organisation the whole truth when he infiltrates it? Must he introduce himself as a police agent sent among them in order to spy?

Can a Christian belong to a research team in psychology or social science?

Researchers had to find out how teacher expectations affect student achievement. For this purpose psychologists told eighteen elementary school teachers that certain children in their class would bloom academically while others probably would not. They said they had predicted the children's success on the basis of test scores. Actually, there was no difference among the children. But by the end of the year, the researchers found what they had predicted. The children who were expected by their teachers to succeed scored higher than those who were not. An important psychological factor had been established statistically: the expectation of success that a teacher has for a child helps this child to progress. But the psychologists had not told the teachers the truth. Harsh men would call them deceivers.

Similar procedures are used in double-blind studies in

medicine, which are considered essential to the discovery of 'truth' regarding a new drug or treatment.

Can a Christian be a businessman? Can he use advertising? Can he claim that his lotion or his shoes are the best? When did he check all the lotions of the world to find out that his is the best? But how can he advertise without praising his product and comparing it to others?

Jesus said that he is not only the truth, but the truth and the life. Truth has its rights, and necessities of life have their rights. You cannot demand absolute truthfulness when by practising it you jeopardise the eternal destiny of hundreds of millions of men held captive by satanic Communism.

If it is wrong to avoid the truth in all circumstances, it must be wrong to steal too.

Flag of Youth, appearing in Moscow, recounted the story of Sister Sitch, whose child Slava was taken from her by sentence of court because she taught him that atheists are sons of the devil and instructed him to keep his eyes closed when motion pictures mocking religion were shown in school. Sister Sitch 'stole' her own child from the atheistic boarding school, and sent him to brethren in Vitebsk, where he was hidden. (The neighbours were told that he was an orphan.) The authorities discovered 'the delinquent' and took him back. But his mother sometimes succeeds in meeting him secretly.

Her second child was also taken away from her, after he had violently torn down the Soviet emblem and told the teacher that he pitied her because she is godless and will burn in hell.

Did Sister Sitch do wrong to steal her own child? Is it theft to take back your child who has been kidnapped by the Communists? Perhaps it is rather the Communists who are the thieves.

I wonder who are the liars. Is it the Bible-smugglers or the Communists who deceive people with atheism and ban the Word of God, or perhaps our critics who are sticklers for morals in matters they do not comprehend.

In 1 Corinthians 9:22 St Paul expresses his determination to save some men 'by all means'. If he says 'by all means', who has the right to correct him, stating that salvation should be propagated only through legal or 'moral' means?

For me the important thing is that our Bibles arrive.

Your contributions make it possible to send literature into Communist countries. Aeroplanes sometimes drop literature on Cuba. Communist radar cannot detect aeroplanes that fly accompanied by angels.

I was filled with joy when we received news that our sea packages had arrived as intended. The first confirmation was received from Soviet brethren of German extraction who were allowed to emigrate to West Germany. One of them told us how they had heard the announcement over the radio with the code word taken from Ecclesiastes: 'Throw your bread upon the waters, and you will find it after many days.' They began to watch along the shore. The Communist police, warned by Judases, also waited. But they got tired, whereas our brethren did not. They continued to watch. On the fourth day the Gospels arrived. Brethren took them from the Baltic shore as far as the Russian-Chinese frontier.

Later radio Tirana began to swear at us, proof that the Gospel tracts had arrived at their Albanian shore. The peak of joy in this regard was the first letter we received from Red China confirming that Gospel tracts sent on the waves had reached the hands of believers.

My greatest satisfaction is that the book which teaches how to get a compassionate heart towards fellowmen, an ardent one for the Lord and a steel one towards one's self, is now penetrating the gates of the Iron Curtain countries.

Another reproach brought against us is that some men suffer for smuggling the Word of God into Communist countries. Many who spread the literature secretly were apprehended. Others, who were converted due to our literature, went to prison or had their children taken away from them.

Before us, the Lord Jesus had the same problem. He warned his disciples that if they followed his way they would be persecuted. He said, 'I send you as sheep among wolves,' which means to certain death. Was it right for him to do so? If they had not become disciples of his, the apostles would have lived long lives and died peaceable deaths. Instead, almost all experienced prison and martyrdom. Was it right for St Paul to bring to conversion men in Rome, knowing that the Emperor Nero would throw them to the wild beasts for their faith?

We are in the same situation.

We love people with the ultimate love, that for their souls. The Word of God can save souls for eternity. Without it, souls are lost, so every risk must be taken in the fight to snatch souls from the fires of hell.

Relief work for the families of Christian martyrs is also very risky. It usually goes smoothly thanks to the many precautions we take. An accident can happen here, too. People can go to prison for helping families of martyrs. Should we give up this too, because it is risky and can't be done openly?

We will not give more details about our smuggling work. I have asked God in prayer that the shadow of my good deeds, if I do any, should always fall behind me.

Smuggling out material

We smuggle not only into Communist countries, we also smuggle out. An enormous amount of material proving the existence of the contested Underground Church and its suffering has arrived in the West.

The Communists themselves have given up denying its existence. They even acknowledge its unbelievable size, despite sixty years of anti-Christian terrorism. A Soviet author, Teplianov, writes in his book, *The Problems of Atheist Education* (Voronej University Press) that in the district of Voronej alone there are 48 authorised and 482 underground Orthodox churches, plus 23 of the 'the True Orthodox Christians', a branch of Orthodoxism. There are 8 official and 97 underground Baptist churches, one official and 14 unofficial churches of the Old-Rite Orthodox, and so on. The number of underground churches is ten times that of the churches whose leadership has compromised with the Communists.

The Soviet newspaper *Kazakhstanskaia Pravda*, reported that brethren in the Soviet Union print great quantities of Christian literature themselves. Sister Vershtshaghina from Alma-Ata, Ivan and Maria Pavliutchenko, Valentina Maximova and Tamara Sokova were all arrested because they arranged the printing of thousands of Christian hymnbooks in a Soviet State printing shop. They had the connivance of the director and all the workers and drivers, and no one denounced them. So much does the average Soviet citizen sympathise with Christianity, even if he does not belong to an underground church.

The production of these hymnbooks cost the Christians of Alma-Ata 10,000 roubles, the salary of a worker for 100 months. Its equivalent in the West would be £20,000. Which of the opulent churches of Britain could easily raise such a sum? The Christians of the Soviet Union are poor, yet they can afford to give an average of 40 per cent of their income to the church. No money is spent on luxurious buildings, choir robes, cookies after the service and so on. Everything goes towards the propagation of the Gospel. Proportionally, they give far more for the spreading of Christian literature than we, in the West, give to help with it. And when caught, they give up their liberties and sometimes their lives, too.

So much the Soviets have discovered. So much we report. We never report any Underground Church activity unless 'the offenders' have already been caught. But it is safe to say that secret printing of Christian literature within Communist countries goes on in many places. Those involved in the printing must sometimes live as if entombed beneath the earth. In this case, to avoid betrayal, they must not leave their subterranean prison which is without sun, flowers, or families, but which they freely choose out of love for God's word and the people who need it. The printers are imprisoned in their secret printing shop. This is how members of a church aflame serve the Lord.

Somewhere a church was burning down. Among the spectators was a well-known atheist. The pastor told him, 'While the church was in good condition you did not attend it. But now, when it is on fire, you come.' The atheist replied, 'If your church had always been on fire, I would have attended regularly.' Set your church aflame through union with the heroic Underground Church and through helping it.

Many were upset because our organisation discounted the top leaders of the churches in Communist countries (except Poland, Yugoslavia and East Germany) as usually being traitors and cat's-paws of the Reds. (Of course, there are many honourable exceptions.)

Was I right to call them such names? In the first place, men have different temperaments and speak accordingly. Peter, mentioning Judas in Acts 1:16, does not call him traitor, but John calls him both traitor and thief. Each had his own way of expressing himself. Temperaments are as little a matter for debate as tastes in food. Secondly, no organisation which does something practical to help behind the Iron Curtain, and is knowledgeable in Communist methods, can consider the official leadership of churches other than as I consider them.

Father Werenfried Van Straaten, head of the Catholic organisation, Aid to the Church in Need, writes, 'We have no right to believe the declaration of Soviet prelates who can visit us because they are agents of Moscow. One of the most dangerous among them is the Metropolitan Nikodeme, forty-one years of age, who, being Komsomolist, was suddenly ordained priest without ever having been in a cloister or seminary. Without any theological preparation, he was at twenty-eight years of age already a bishop. As a mighty man in the Moscow patriarchate, he has been systematically destroying the Orthodox Church for eleven years. According to the unchallengeable proofs of Andre Martin, Nikodeme is the evil spirit which organises the suicide of Orthodoxy with genial perversity, while he gives the Vatican quieting statements about religious liberty in the Soviet Union. Faithfulness to the persecuted church obliges us to unmask this bishop, who has the closing of 15,000 churches on his conscience.'

What Fr Van Straaten said about the late Metropolitan Nikodeme also applies to others.

The 30th Apostolic canon and canon 3 of the 2nd Nicean Ecumenical Council state: 'If any bishop, making use of secular powers, shall by these means obtain jurisdiction over any church, he shall be deposed and also excommunicated together with all those who remain in communion with him.'

The Church condemned the legal interference of secular power and the secular appointment of a bishop at a time when the rulers themselves were Christians! How much more severely must she condemn it when the rulers are militant Satanists!

'Charity . . . does not behave unseemly' (1 Cor. 13:5). These words are usually understood to mean that a Christian does not behave impolitely. But St Paul himself was sometimes terribly impolite. So was the Lord. So were the reformers and their opponents. Where the fate of the Church, indeed, of the world, is at stake, politeness can do great harm.

The Greek word for 'unseemly' is *aschemon*. A literal translation of this passage would therefore be, 'charity does not behave without a scheme'.

Christ categorises men exactly like a zoologist, framing them in a system, in a scheme. Some men are 'sheep', others 'wolves', others 'dogs', others 'foxes'. Some He calls fools, hypocrites and vipers. Others are beloved disciples. He knows a beast, a red dragon and a chosen dove. Love does not behave unseemly, that is, without having this scheme in view.

All men must be loved, but I cannot treat the 'sheep' like the 'wolf', nor can I behave with hypocrites as I would with beloved disciples, with tyrants as with victims. Woe to the shepherd who cannot distinguish between sheep and wolves, and who would behave similarly towards a good and a bad husband, an obedient and a disobedient child. The attitude of charity depends upon the situation.

If a group of gangsters attack an innocent man, I love them all, but I try to protect the innocent man, shooting if necessary at the gangsters. Otherwise my behaviour would be unseemly, or *aschemon*, not taking into account the fact that in the scheme of the world they occupy different positions. The same holds true in our attitude towards those who benefit the Church and those who harm it. Our mission violently attacks any church leaders whose aim is to destroy the Church.

Having recounted some of the many objections brought against us, I can now write about some other aspects of our work.

Our organisation broadcasts the Gospel in twelve languages spoken in Communist countries or countries endangered by Communism. This effort has brought us many strange responses.

A listener from Shanghai asked, 'I am an atheist. But I know that in the curriculum of foreign countries there is one subject called "theology" or "the study of the soul". What does it say? Will you explain it to me? . . . When men die, their spirits also expire. So, they won't be a spirit in fact. I don't understand that Jesus is God and that God follows what we do.'

Another listener, Ye-Chen, wrote, 'Time passes like flowing water. I don't know if man's life is a limited one.'

And another: 'Is the patience towards bad actions a good thing for a Christian?' This is a typical question.

The most touching Chinese letter is one from a young man in Canton: 'As I listen to the programme broadcast by your radio I begin to know Jesus Christ. I am a believer. But what does it mean to be a believer when men are entirely separated from God, having no church inbetween? [All the churches of Red China were closed then.] Indeed, I don't know what it is to pray. Perhaps it is that after all things we said, we should be able to add the words "Amen".' (Could we add an 'Amen' after every word of ours?)

This is the best definition of prayer I have ever heard. Let me exemplify this young man's teaching:

You come home from work, tired and irritated. Your wife brings you supper, but it does not taste good. No salt in it. In exchange, one of her hairs floats on the surface of the soup. You can bully your wife, 'What kind of a soup is this? Why are you not more careful? Look here, it is dirty. A hair is floating in it. Did you comb yourself while cooking? I hope you will never do this again.' Try to say an 'Amen' after this. It does not fit. But, you can proceed otherwise. You can tell her, 'I really appreciate that you are still in love as in the first days we knew each other. Thinking about me, you forgot to put salt in the soup. But you atoned for this with a nice surprise. You know how I love your beautiful hair. What a good idea to put a hair in the soup. Tomorrow I will buy a medallion and put the hair in it. Then I will keep it forever around my neck. No need to put hair in the soup in the future. And now, give me a really big hug.' If you speak like this to your wife, you can add 'Amen'.

This manner of prayer is the fulfilment of the commandment, 'Pray unceasingly.' I learned it from a Chinese teenager whom we wished to teach the Gospel to over the radio.

In 1944, when I started the secret missionary work among the Soviet soldiers who had invaded Romania, I saw that, although I spoke Russian, I had no language in common with them. When I told them the parable of the man who had a hundred sheep and lost one, they objected, 'No man can have one hundred sheep. They belong to the collective.' When I told them about the workers of the vineyard who refused to give the owner the fruit, killing his servants and his son, their reply was, 'These husbandmen did well to rebel. The owner of the vineyard was a landlord and his property had to be confiscated.' They laughed about the Virgin Mary: 'Why should a girl be a virgin?' And 'King Jesus?' They had the worst opinion of kings. They had no idea what Pharisees, Sadducees, Herodians, temple, altar, tithe, psalms, Holy Spirit, or even angels were. It was impossible for them to understand a Gospel, even if they had it in their own language.

For this reason I wrote a 'Gospel in Marxist Language'. As St Matthew had told the story of Jesus to the Jews, and St Luke to the Greeks, I told it to the Communists, explaining the Gospel to them in a way they could understand.

These special broadcasts made the Communist press furious. We had the honour of being the religious radio programme most attacked by the Soviets.

A Pentecostal pastor from Russia was allowed to emigrate and is now in the USA. He told us how Christians were called to the Soviet Secret Police and asked to write letters to the Far East Broadcasting Company. The letters were clever. They complimented the radio station for doing Christ's work, and asked it to continue because the Word was so highly appreciated. The letters complained of only one thing. The believers allegedly did not like 'The Gospel translated into Marxist language'. This is what happens when you step on an adversary's toes.

The Gospel translated into Marxist language also had exceptional effects in the free world. We broadcast it in Spanish, and received a letter from a Peruvian guerrilla. This man had heard it in the bush, gun in hand. He was struck by Jesus' teaching about loving your enemies, and in the twinkle of an eye his heart was changed. He realised at once how foolish it was to handle murderous weapons. He left the jungle, went to the city, joined a church and became a Sunday school teacher. Still, he had no rest in his heart. After two years he dropped everything and returned to the bush to bring Christ to his former comrades. We never heard from him again. He was probably killed by the other Communists who must have considered him a traitor.

In response to our broadcasts in Romanian, a sister wrote from there, 'I thank the heavenly Father and the Lord Jesus for you, because we are fed with the Holy Word, which we hear on the radio from your mouth. I awake during the night and kneel, asking God to give you health and power that we might continue to hear your voice.'

The children of this world are often cleverer than the children of light. Two thousand years ago the chief priests knew the value of the mass media. They knew Pilate to be, like all men, suggestible. A great multitude could influence him to do things which he would have shunned had he pondered them quietly in solitude. Mass suggestion is a great power. The high priests used a mass demonstration to manipulate Pilate. But mass suggestion can also be used for good.

If we wish to bring the news of salvation to the Communist world, to help Christian martyrs, to make known the heroism of the Underground Church; if we wish the free countries to be informed about what Communism really is and how it can be overcome by Christ, we have to cry aloud. This is what we do through radio.

The questions put by listeners in the Soviet Union are heart-rending: 'Why does man die? From where does death come? What is the meaning of death? What is communion with God and how can we have it? I ask you to speak slowly and repeat the answers to my questions for I will copy down the answers.'

Communist authorities are alarmed about our broadcasts, which shows that we are on the right track. But religious broadcasting exists not only from abroad. *Novoe R. Slovo* writes about religious programmes which are spread over secret radio stations within the Soviet Union. The penalty for this is death.

This work deals a deadly blow to all who have contested the existence of an Underground Church. Br Garfield Williams, secretary of the European Conference of Churches, wrote in the Swiss newspaper *Gazette De Lausanne* that the notion of the Underground Church was 'badly defined, generalised and exaggerated'. I have shown in my books that the Russian Underground Church has secret academies, secret prayer meetings and baptisms, secret ordinations of pastors and bishops, secret infiltrators in Communist ranks (considered afterwards by the Communists as traitors), secret magazines, secret printing presses, secret convents. If all these do not suffice to prove that an Underground Church exists, there is still one more characteristic: secret radio emitters. If I can prove that a man has a living body, a soul and a spirit and this is not enough to convince Br Williams that he is a human being, then I can do nothing more for him.

Agitator, a Moscow magazine, bitterly attacked the Christian broadcasting which 'fills the ether with broadcasts whose aim is the increase of interest towards religion, the inciting of religious fanaticism and [here they hit the nail on the head] the transformation of religious views and inclinations in a union and solidarity against the Socialist regime.' They say that the teachings contained in these broadcasts are taken by preachers and believers as rules of life. Russian brethren tell us, 'Your sermons are balm for our souls. They are a glass of cold water in the scorching hot desert of this world.'

Pravda Ukraini rightly complains that the aim of our broadcasts is to softly lead the believers to pass in an unobserved manner from opposing the materialist outlook to political opposition towards the Soviet State.

The Soviet State does not accept the words of Jesus 'Render to Caesar what is Caesar's and to God what is God's.' They demand the whole man for Communism alone. If Caesar has attained such arrogance, Christians owe him nothing.

A recent communication from Soviet believers also contains a message for you, the supporters of our mission: 'We think especially those who take care of the needs of the saints. "I was naked and ye clothed me; I was sick and ye healed me, I was in prison and ye came to me . . . Verily I say unto you, inasmuch as ye have done it unto one of the least of my brethren, ye have done unto me." For the Christian sharing with the sufferers of the Russian church, for the parcels, printed matter and all the other help which He knows, we thank God and you. We ask for all the Christian sympathy. If one member suffers, the whole body suffers. Your reward is with God.'

We assure you that your service for our brethren behind the Iron Curtain is not in vain. There are reports from Romania and from the Soviet Union that at the hour the Gospel is broadcast, everyone in a village leaves what they are doing and gathers in the homes of those who have a radio. Unbelievers as well as Christians gather together and listen kneeling to the sermon. Even high-ranking Communists are converted through Christian broadcasts from abroad.

Helping families of martyrs

Your contributions are used for sending parcels to Christian martyrs. One such family which received a parcel wrote, 'We shouted with such a shout of joy that you heard it in America.'

A Baptist pastor's wife who was left to keep eight children when her husband was sentenced wrote 'I received your parcel. I thank God that he has given me the privilege to bear a chip of the cross of Christ. The children ask when father will return. But their daddy has been to the stake for the faith once delivered to the saints.'

Another letter is signed by the President of the Baptist

Union of the Soviets, Kriutchkov, who is in hiding, having a warrant of arrest issued against him for his faith: 'Thanks for the Christian books and your broadcasts. Our spiritual hunger is not stilled yet, but through your endeavours we have been saved from spiritual starvation.' We have many such letters.

We split the Communist parties

We also had some completely unexpected successes, the greatest of which was that in the process of uncovering Communist crimes, we split the Communist parties.

Figaro, Paris of 12 December, 1976, wrote that Mr Paul Klavins, co-worker of our German mission, smuggled out of the Soviet Union a movie about the prison of Krosvstpilz-Ella in Riga (Soviet Latvia). We gave the film to the American (CBS), British, French and other television stations which showed it. As a result, *Humanité*, organ of the French Communist Party, protested against the bad treatment of the prisoners. Although *Pravda* angrily denied the film's authenticity, its authenticity was confirmed by another Soviet magazine *Literaturnaia Gazeta* on 24 December.

The *Los Angeles Times* of 3 November, 1976, disclosed that the Soviet Communist Party sent a long letter to the leading Communist parties in the Western world, mainly discussing this film which our mission had succeeded in smuggling to the West.

In this document the Soviets defensively tried to explain the film away by asserting that Soviet studies showed 15 per cent of their prisoners to be insane. Of course that did not explain whether this insanity occurred before imprisonment or after it. This letter decisively proves how effective our mission's work is.

After participating in a press conference given by Br Klavins, director of our French mission, and Sister Grossu, French newspapers, including the Communist ones, unanimously condemned the Red terror. The British Communists also dissociated themselves from the Soviets. Things went so far that the general secretary of the French Communist Party, Marchais, did not attend an International

Communist Convention in the Soviet Union. The Italian Communist Party also publicly condemned the cruel practices of their Soviet comrades. We have opened the eyes of some Communists in the West by exposing atrocities committed by their Soviet confrères. Our publicity makes it more difficult for others to come to power and do the same things.

6: Milestones

At an International Conference

A highlight in the history of our mission was its first international conference at Chateau d'Oex in Switzerland. Representatives from all continents were present. Since we are a secret organisation, I cannot disclose much of what we discussed and decided there, but what impressed me most was the full love and understanding among our directors.

The conference sent a cable to Hodder and Stoughton, publishers of my books, thanking them for being the first secular publishing house in history to be a main factor in constituting a world-wide Christian mission.

I have retained two other strong impressions from that conference. One was the ordination of my son, now general director of the United States mission, by the Norwegian Lutheran bishop, Nonderval, seconded by pastors of nine nationalities, including myself. I had prayed during the long years in prison that he should belong to the Lord. And he does.

The second impression was from the Holy Communion we took together. Not having a congregation of my own to lead, I almost never give Communion. This time I had to deliver the sermon. While I knelt in prayer, I understood the sense of Communion as never before.

In it we commemorate the death of the Son, but implicitly we remember the Father who sent him into the world for this purpose. Scripture says, 'It pleased the Lord to bruise Him' (Isa. 53:3). We commemorate the anguish of the Son and the pleasure which the Father took in it.

The Triune God created the world. When iron was created, the Father told the Son, 'Of iron like this the nails will be made which will be driven into your hands and feet.' When trees were made the Father said, 'From such a tree, the cross on which you will hang will be fashioned, so also will the beams of the temple.' Animals were endowed with skin from which would be made shoes but also the leather whips wherewith the Son will be flogged. Then man was created, with thousands of nerves to sense joy, but also that Jesus might be able to suffer excruciating pain.

I remembered the words of a Communist torturer, 'If there is a God we fulfil His will by torturing you. If God created the human body, he created it chiefly in order that it should suffer pain. How many zones are there in the body the touch of which produces pleasure? Five or six. But as for torture, I can do it by making girls hang by their hair or by beating them on their soles. There is not an inch of the human body which cannot feel pain.'

The Father made the lachrymal gland, telling Christ, 'This is for your mother, so that she may weep on Golgotha.' What a phrase: 'It pleased the Lord to bruise him!' He made human blood to be shed for just causes. All its other uses are subsidiary.

At this Communion I bowed before the mystery of God as never before.

If there were no tension within the perfect unity of Godhead, why the need to stress the oneness? Those who are simply one have no need to assert it.

I remembered the strange words of the Lord in John 16:7, 'If I go not away, the Comforter [the Holy Spirit] will not come unto you.' It seems as if the two avoid meeting with the same man in the same place.

I could sense something of what appears to us as a tension within the Holy Trinity, because I, too, belong to the family of God and there is tension between God and myself who loves Him. If there were perfect harmony, why would we all require from God so many things which do not flow spontaneously from His heart? The usual real prayer of believers is 'Let not thy, but *my* will be done,' even though the mouth says otherwise.

I have the impression that in our fight against Communism, we fight against a destiny established by God.

It was God's decision that Hitler rule Germany until its complete destruction. Hitler told Speer, 'Providence helped me,' which was true. It helped him achieve the complete destruction of Germany. Therefore all attempts on his life failed.

Revelation 12 tells us about a dragon to whom God gave the power to make war with the saints and to overcome them. 'Power was given him [by whom else, if not by God?] over all kindreds and tongues and nations.'

I cannot bear Communists taking over almost half the world. I will have to accept worse things. The Church will be defeated temporarily as Jesus was defeated on Golgotha.

I pray like the Lord in Gethsemane that this cup may pass, but it will not. Only in the end whosoever hates Zion will be put to shame by God. They will be destroyed in the fire like grass. This is the song of the Orthodox Church in Russia.

I understand nothing. Reason tells me that the whole thing is absurd. I gave up what Luther called 'the beast of reason'; I believed and worshipped.

We held our second international conference in Jerusalem. This time we had representatives from countries as far away as Japan, Vietnam (it was the last time we saw our Vietnamese director. He chose to stay when the South fell to the Communists and is probably no more among the living), Peru, Colombia, Brazil, Australia and Finland.

It had become an absolute necessity for us to meet and confer together. But how could we gather such an international conference without spending a great deal of money? We decided to convene in Jerusalem, and thus we were able to combine our conference with an international tour to the Holy Land with some 250 participants from different countries. For a certain number of tickets sold, we received one free. That way our directors cost us nothing.

Visiting sites where Jesus lived has remained an unforgettable experience for us all. But one thing surpassed even that. We had among us Brother Klaassen, who survived ten years in Communist prisons, Brother Hamm, who was deported to the Arctic Circle for twenty years, and Brother Rose, who had his own story of persecution. To watch these men seeing Israel was an excitement apart.

Since I had been in Israel previously, I met innumerable old friends from my former Hebrew Christian congregation in Romania who had emigrated to Israel after my imprisonment. I also met the former officer of the Communist Secret Police who had been helpful in my release from prison. He had been jailed for having done his best to free me. On the day when he had finished his term, he came to me with a flower, 'This, as token of gratitude that you gave me the opportunity to suffer for so glorious a cause.'

We also established our missionary work in Israel. My books appeared in Hebrew and Arabic. The latter edition has been sent into Arab states. Several other international conferences followed.

New stratagems to confuse minds

The problems which face us are constantly changing. When I first arrived in the West, Communist persecution was flatly denied by many leftists in the news media and even in the Church. This line is no more tenable now, but another tactic has been adopted. Some organisations minimise Communist persecution and drown it in a jumble of news about injustices in the free world: dictatorships in South Korea, military governments in Latin America and racism in South Africa. The major Communist threat becomes lost in a multitude of unjust imprisonments that exist everywhere in the world. Institutes for research of events in Communist countries were created and the churches eased their consciences by supporting the research projects. The Church of England, the Lutheran Church of Germany and Norway, the Episcopalian and Lutheran Churches of the United States of America (Missouri Synod) made resolutions in favour of oppressed Christians.

But research alone – though valuable – does not help the oppressed. The Jews do not develop research: they fight for their co-religionists and support them. It is good to find out how many prisoners there are in Russia, it is more important to feed them, whether they be 300 or 30,000. The whole intellectual world stood up for one unjustly imprisoned Jew, Dreyfuss – they did not wait to determine whether there was a second, or whether they had spelled his name correctly.

Children of martyrs cannot eat resolutions taken in their favour. They need bread.

There can be no comparison between Communist atrocities and other abuses which exist throughout the world. Show me something comparable to the Gulag Archipelago in any other country. Show me a regime which has killed tens of millions of its citizens under such indescribable tortures. Has South Africa killed a million blacks? In South Korea, Billy Graham preached freely to a million people – it was the largest Christian gathering in history.

Injustices and abuses exist everywhere, it is true. But Communism is intrinsically evil. It is satanic. I proved in my book *Was Karl Marx A Satanist?* the direct connections between the founder of modern Communism and a sect of devil-worshippers.

The Soviet Union is the only country in the world in which the fable about ritual murder is still perpetrated.

In the book *Children and Religion,* the Communists reiterate the old lie that Christians teach and practice ritual murder; that to atone for their sins, they kill their own children. The Romans said it nineteen centuries ago, and now the Communists tell this story to children in order to frighten them out of becoming Christians.

Documents of the renowned Odessa trial of Baptists in 1969 charged them with cutting the veins of one to be baptised and drinking the blood. Not since Nero's time have such mad lies been told about Christians.

In *Who Are The Pentecostals?* (published by Ananie, Moscow), it is told that in the village of Litkino, a Christian woman named Smirnova killed one of her young sons and maimed another as a sacrifice to God; a Christian named Lazko is accused of having killed his seven-year-old daughter with an axe to glorify God.

Another accusation of ritual murder is made in Davidchenko's book, *What Believers are Taught in the Sects* (published by Bielorus). A Baptist named Mudrii allegedly killed his brother in accordance with Baptist teachings.

In the book *We Must Not Forget About,* by F. Dolgich and A. Kurantov, issued by the Military Publishing House of Moscow, we read, 'The sectarian of the religious congregation of Karaganda, Anna Nevelinaia, brought her son aged six as a sacrifice to God. She threw herself with him before a train.' The truth behind this story is probably that the court had decided to take Nevelinaia's son away from her, because she taught him about Christ. Fearing that the Communists would make him godless, she resorted to this desperate act, which is beyond human judgment.

The same book reports that in the village of Neftgorsk, Pastor M. Krivolapov decided to 'sacrifice to God a lamb without blemish, the three-year-old son of the sectarian Osiovetz. The pastor killed the child in the presence of his mother and all the worshippers, none of whom even attempted to prevent the terrible crime because they considered it to be the will of the Holy Spirit. The child was afterwards buried at night in a dark forest.' His young mother died of grief – the father had already died as a result of prolonged fasting.

The book explains that pastor Krivolapov's act fulfilled Christ's commandment that we renounce our relatives in order to be his disciples.

In the Moscow newspaper *Znamia Tunosti*, Baptists are accused of having killed a girl, Vania Voinelovich, by means of baptism. Baptism, say the Communists, leads to pneumonia. This girl fell sick, thus the pastor who baptised her is guilty of murder.

These are only a few stories which have leaked through the Iron Curtain – how many more such insane charges against our brethren in Russia must there be about which we never hear!

Atrocities in Red China

The Hong Kong *Star* quoted a businessman returning from Shanghai, Communist China's largest city, who said he witnessed the fatal torturing of a Chinese Roman Catholic. 'He said, "They grabbed him and took him to a school on the outskirts where they formed a twenty-man court of high school students. He was charged and found guilty of neglecting his prime duty by not knowing Mao's thoughts and choosing religion instead . . . The victim wore a crucifix." The businessman said the teenage crowd wanted to crucify the Chinese believer. The Red Guards pelted him with eggs and stones, then tortured him with hot pokers. His screams were heard by passers-by.'

Another Chinese Christian was found with a Bible hidden

in a pillow. For this he was stripped naked, smeared with honey, and made to stand in the fierce sun for many hours.

Vart Land (Norway), reported that in Swatow a pastor was dragged through the streets wearing a dunce's cap which had ugly inscriptions on it. In Red China, clergy could be executed for refusing to chant the Red book of Mao Tse-Tung before their flocks.

The suffering of the Chinese Church surpasses all imagination. The Catholics announce that over a million of them have been killed (Dauriac, *Requiem for the Church of China*). We do not have the figure for the Protestants, but it must be proportional.

Dr D. Rees, former missionary in China, returning from a fact-finding tour, wrote to us, 'All my Chinese friends have been killed or imprisoned. One was blinded, one thrown into a well, two died of tuberculosis, and another, when brainwashed, went out of his mind and signed a recantation. When his reason returned, he tore up the recantation. But the Chinese Christian Church is growing by thousands. It is called *Pi keo wuyen tib Chiao huei* (The Church of Closed Lips). No one speaks to another, but neighbours are converted through the operation of the Holy Spirit. All my Chinese friends of the Jesus Family (Watchman Nee's denomination) have been done to death by various means, thousands of them.'

An Indian doctor, Kuman Chandah, had his legs cut and his eyes gouged out in one of Red China's prisons.

In one such incident, Valdimir Tatishtshev, a Russian, was arrested in Shanghai. The Chinese torturers tied iron tubes to his legs with screws and hammered on them until his bones were broken, to make him confess imaginary crimes. When he refused, the Communist police went to his home. An officer picked up Tatishtshev's baby and told the mother, 'If you don't sign an accusation against your husband, we will smash your child's head in.' The mother, stunned and unbelieving, refused. Then the police officer, a woman herself, smashed the baby's head against the wall. The mother stabbed the officer, and the other Communists shot the mother.

Radio Moscow said on 7 April, 1970, 'In the course of ten years, more than 25 million people in China were exterminated . . . The discontented were dumped by the million into enormous concentration camps.'

The Moscow newspaper *Krasnaia Zvezda*, on 7 May, 1969, wrote, 'The Chinese Communist Party . . . have burned people's eyes out with boiling water and sulphuric acid, hacked off limbs with penknives and split open skulls with stones and ancient broadswords.'

Many of our Chinese brethren are groping now in blindness or creeping on their bellies, their limbs having been hacked off. The Bible teaches us in Hebrews 13:3 to remember their sufferings as if we suffered with them. Do you?

The hope that the Communist regime will become more humane is an illusion. Some 'liberty' granted recently is just a tactical move. The few open churches are served by a clergy which has compromised with Communism. The underground church is mushrooming. It is best to keep silent about our intense missionary work in China.

My intention was to write about the mission which I founded, about myself and my years in the free world. But where in the world is this 'myself'? It is well for men to remember that psychology has not yet discovered any clear-cut tangible reference for the term personality, any distinct subject for investigation that can be isolated and accurately assessed. What would be the purpose of a personality separated from the cause to which its life pertains? Cannot a personality be so intensified as to comprehend all the suffering of China and much more?

Intending to write about myself, I wrote about China and the whole Communist camp. To me this does not seem at all incongruous.

If I seemingly deviated, let me do it completely by describing the manner in which Chinese Christians respond to these atrocities.

It is stupid to fear those who can kill only the body, instead of fearing the one who can throw both body and soul in Gehenna. A sword was put to the chest of a Christian and he was asked, 'Are you a Christian?' When he answered, 'Yes,' they would have killed him, but an officer said, 'Free him, he is an idiot.' Someone asked him later, 'How could you confess Christ with such courage?' and his reply was, 'I read the story of Peter's denial of Christ and I did not wish to weep bitterly.'

Among the many stories about our martyred Chinese brethren is this eye-witness report about the stoning to death of a Christian girl in a Communist labour camp. The girl was bound hand and foot and made to kneel in the centre of a circle of people who were commanded to stone her. Those who refused were shot. She died with her face shining like St Stephen. At least one of those present was led to faith in Christ through this girl who sealed her testimony with her blood. A young man prayed for his persecutors as he hung six days on a cross before dying. Five students who were sent out to dig deep holes into which they were to be thrown, sang Christian hymns as they were buried alive.

What is the solution?

Most people agree with my criticism of Communism: they sympathise with the suffering, but they ask me, 'What is the solution?'

Mankind's greatest traumas were produced by those who believed they had solutions. Marx, Hitler and Stalin believed they had answers to burning questions. All those who have drawn mankind into world wars, revolutions, and struggles for independence which resulted in worse slavery, believed they possessed solutions. I believe that the future is sealed up with God, and that we are not meant to foresee it: except for a few prophetic glimpses, mankind progresses along an unknown path.

I know that the answer will not satisfy everyone, but I can only recommend the same solution given by Jesus: Love everyone, love even the Communists and try to bring them to Christ. That is what our mission does.

A traveller wearing a funny overcoat walked along a road. The sun and the wind made a wager about which of them would succeed in making him take off his coat. First the wind blew as fiercely as it could. It was an icy wind, and the more it blew, the more closely the wanderer wrapped himself in his coat. Then the sun began to shine first mildly, then warmer and warmer. The traveller took off the overcoat, folded it and put it on his arm. Warm love succeeds where anti-Communist attacks do not.

Our first great weapon is the love we show, not only to the victims of Communism, but also to their Communist oppressors.

Our second great weapon is self-sacrifice.

'There are hundreds of ways to obtain God's love, but only one is sure,' said a preacher. 'What's that?' asked a colleague. 'Aha,' retorted the first. 'I thought you wouldn't know.'

The least known way to obtain God's love is the simplest one: to keep his commandments. The Lord Jesus said, 'He that has my commandments, and keeps them, he it is that loves me; and he that loves me shall be loved by my Father, and I will love him' (John 14:21). He also said, 'If you will enter into life, keep the commandments' (Matt. 19:17). Every morning sing a hymn, read a Bible portion, pray, have a quiet time to listen to what God has to say to you that day, and then set about fulfilling his commands.

His many commandments could be resolved into one: to imitate him, even though this might involve suffering and possibly death.

Jesus died for the glory of the Father and commands all his disciples to die to sin (Rom. 6:2), and to lose, if necessary, their natural life in obedience to the commandments. A religion is truly religion if you are ready to die for it. A belief that is not worthy of the sacrifice of life is not religion. The desire to lead a consistent Christian life can lead to renunciation and painful loss. Do not consider yourself a Christian if this is too great a price for you. Jesus was ready to die on a cross at the age of thirty-four, and we are meant to imitate him in dedication to God and love towards our fellowmen. Whoever keeps his commandment is his beloved.

The Church enjoins a heroic Christian life. One of the names of Jesus is 'Heroic God' (Isa. 9:6 in Hebrew).

We are the only mission behind the Iron Curtain whose associates have been martyred. Brother Kiwanuka, our Ugandan trustee, has been killed, and Brother Wang-Shiu-Mei was beaten to death while trying to smuggle Bibles into

Red China. Our co-workers Jon Clipa and Sabin Teodasiu were killed in Romania.

The blood of the martyrs remains potent and will nourish the Church behind the Iron Curtain, as well as those who support it from the free world. The bloodless sacrifices of those who help them are also of vital importance to the growth of the Underground Church.

Christian prisoners have the right to be visited twice a year, but the way from Minsk to Siberia is long and costly. Families of prisoners cannot obtain jobs. The Communists hope that believers will renounce their faith, if not because of self-love, at least in order to protect their families. Your help strengthens Christians in their determination to keep the commandments and to continue the fight. Jesus died on the cross, but he could rely on the fact that the apostle John would take care of his mother. The Christians in Communist prisons, too, can suffer and die quietly when they know that you will not forsake their families.

Our anniversary

The seal that the world puts on the foreheads of its elect is success and popularity. These are of no great value to the children of God.

A recent poll showed that the most popular politician in Italy is Berlinguer, leader of the Communist Party, a Marxist-Leninist, and therefore a man committed to duplicity. In order to abolish religion and morality (see K. Marx, *Communist Manifesto*). Berlinguer presently disguises himself as a democrat. Lenin, too, called himself a social-democrat until he came to power; then he began the slaughter of millions of innocents.

During the long night through which mankind passes, Hitler and Stalin were also popular. So are many phoney religious leaders, who despise the church established by Christ, and attract followers by playing on people's sentiments and exciting them. Man can get excited about anything, but jubilation in the truth is what really counts.

Fifteen years have passed since we founded our mission. we started by publicising a very unpopular cause. But daring to stand for the truth when it is unpopular is the seal of God.

We knew that, on the whole, men care little about martyrs dying for Christ in countries far away. What do they care about a billion souls under Communist rule who are forcibly kept away from Christ; the only source of salvation? Who weeps at the thought that these souls may go to eternal damnation? Men are seldom deeply touched by tragedies that exist at the other end of the world.

We brought into the apathetic free world the message that the Gospel must be preached in Communist countries, and also among the revolutionists in free states. We had no illusions about success.

Each week about a million people die without knowing about Christ. The world's population increases at the rate of 47 million each year. In this situation, the missionary endeavour of the universal Church is dwindling although we know the Lord's command, 'Go and teach all nations' (Matt. 28:19).

Love, like light, must always be travelling; man must spend it, give it away. When light does not travel at maximum speed it is not light. Christianity that does not do its utmost to win the world for Christ is not Christianity. What is the worth of a selfish faith which assures my going to heaven but does not stimulate me to seek the salvation of others?

We told the world that the Gospel must be propagated in Communist lands, and we started to do so immediately. We also told the story of the saints persecuted by the Communists, and we started to help the families of prisoners. We ourselves are amazed at our success. We did not expect it.

From its very inception, our mission warned that Communism would expand to new countries. It is 'the Red dragon' (Rev. 12:3) ready to devour the Church. It will never be satiated until the whole world is under its heel. Our prophetic warning has come true. In the short time of our mission's existence, the Communists have taken over the following countries: Vietnam, Cambodia, Laos, S. Yemen, Ethiopia, Benine, Congo-Brazzaville, Mozambique, Angola, Afghanistan, etc.

Our mission observed and noted each takeover, while the rest of the world fell prey to the cunning Communist manoeuvre of keeping people's minds diverted with a few well-intentioned but inefficient Russian dissenters. Protests about a few arrests in Russia and the Sakharov interviews were publicised while the Communists occupied several more countries, slaughtering hundreds of thousands, without the world taking any heed. In America, the Communists kept the public's minds focused on the Watergate scandal while they occupied South-East Asia. The Communists have also become the decisive factor in the political life of Italy and France.

Marxism also infiltrates the free world and is ready to attack it militarily. The Belgian general Glose declared that the Soviet army is capable of occupying West Germany in forty-eight hours. Who will resist its advance towards the Atlantic – France, in which the majority voted for the Socialist-Communist front?

Social democracy is basically Marxist too. Although with other methods, its ultimate aims are those proclaimed by Marx: abolition of all religion and morality. In 1953, 33 per cent of all Cabinet members in Western Europe were Social Democrats. Now it is up to 70 per cent.

Before the appearance of our mission, anti-Communists said, 'The only good Communist is a dead Communist.' We say on the contrary, 'Every converted Communist is a saint.'

Our mission contradicted pro-Communists and anti-Communists alike. From a logical point of view, it should not have succeeded. It did. Its existence and rapid expansion is a miracle of God.

The miracle is the more impressive when you consider how many earnest Christian circles opposed us. Their opinion was that secret work in Communist lands cannot be done without deception, and that it is better to leave a third of the world unevangelised than to lie. We will not quarrel with those who hold this view. Our response is that, 'We have seen another angel' than they have seen. This other angel has sealed us with the seal of God on which it is written, 'Save some by all means' (1 Cor. 9:22), through ordinary or extraordinary methods.

At the beginning of the last century, an unusually intelligent girl by the name of Barry felt the call to become a physician. Because girls were not accepted in universities at that time, she disguised herself as a boy. At the age of ten she passed the exams. At fourteen she was a physician in the army, and in time rose to a high military rank, no one suspecting her sex. She dedicated her life to the medical care of convicts, paupers, lunatics, and lepers, as well as the military of South African and Jamaica. Only at her death was it discovered that she was female (June Rose, *The Perfect Gentleman*, Hutchinson, 1977). If one calls her life a perpetual lie because she pretended to be a man, who should receive the blame: the dedicated physician, or those who made the laws forbidding even exceptionally gifted girls to fulfil their God-given vocation?

The same principle applies to the work of smuggling Christian literature and relief for families of Christian prisoners into Communist countries. Our couriers disguise themselves as tourists, diplomats, sportsmen, newspaper-men, etc. If this is a sin, it is the Communists who are responsible for it. We contest their right to forbid the life-giving Gospel to whole nations, and we defy their laws.

The same principle also applies to our personal life. If marriage partners and friends acted joyously even when they felt depressed, if they smiled at each other even when they felt like weeping, if they were gentle even when indignant, their lives would change much. There exists both a saintly honesty and a saintly acting.

We perform our work of spreading the Gospel and maintaining a Christian attitude towards modern problems, knowing beforehand that we will be misunderstood. For instance, it is difficult to communicate to blacks that the worst white domination is preferable to a Red 'independ-ence', which would be an even more abusive regime, blocking even the salvation of souls. Reds pose as freedom-fighters and those who have not felt their whip are readily seduced into trusting them.

It has also been difficult to make Protestants understand that we must defend and aid imprisoned Catholics, and vice versa.

It is the seal of God to do what he ordains, with or without man's approval. On the occasion of our fifteenth anniversary, we take the opportunity to thank all our co-workers, our directors in many lands, our employees and couriers, prayer partners and contributors, all those who defended us, and those who by opposing us, made us re-think our way through their attacks.

It has not been easy. We have had our moments of gloom, but God comforted us when we received letters like the following from the Soviet Union: 'The priests of the Orthodox Church are almost naked. Some were discovered during a liturgy. They work as bricklayers. They badly needed clothing so that they can change clothes when the Police are on their tracks. These priests care for secret churches from Central Asia to Vladivostok. We have distributed the 50,000 roubles.'

This is one of the practical works of our mission. Yet no work at all would be possible without the practical help given by all our friends and supporters. One friend writes, 'I have included you in my will.' Brethren from a Lutheran church wrote, 'We will try to send you a mile of pennies, or £750. We have already collected £170 in pennies.' Another Lutheran church group told us, 'Never have we been so overwhelmed by the true meaning of the Gospel as when we had the privilege of having you preach in our church. Herewith, £250. We will make this an ongoing responsibility of our congregation.'

Among many other letters are these: 'I am eight years old. I got money for feeding donkeys and send you part of it, 40 pence' (Britain).

'We Mennonites and Reformed had a feast in liberty. We remembered those persecuted and have destined the offering for them' (France).

'After reading R. Wurmbrand's *Tortured for Christ*, I desired to give you all I have. Today I closed my bank account and sent you the balance with much love for my suffering brethren.'

Our anniversary commemorates great progress, but many tasks still lie ahead of us, among them the shaking up of many of the clergy who are careless.

I have had occasion to attend many Christian congresses, and some clergymen, when they hear I am from Romania, congratulate me, 'You can be proud of Nadia Comanici. Romania has the finest athlete in the world. We watched her on TV – when you think that she is only fifteen!' I ask them if they also know the name of some Romanian martyr. No one has.

Let me name but a few: the uniate bishops Suciu, Frentziu, Rusu, Hossu, Aftenie (who died insane because of tortures), the priests Macavei, Pop, Moldovan, Stanescu, etc.

Thomas Aquinas taught anger is a dignified and holy thing when the honour and glory of God are at stake. We are angry about some clergy's indifference towards martyrs. We believe all clergy should spend less time watching sports on TV, and more time reading about the lives of martyrs. The change would be reflected in both their sermons and their daily lives.

The clergy should tell Christians in the free world that all believers share in the blood of the innocent victims of Communism. The Soviet Union built up its dictatorship thanks to the loans, technical aid and wheat from the free world. Eastern Europe was given to the Communists in Yalta by Churchill and Roosevelt, elected by their respective people. No Western people except the United States helped Vietnam fight for its freedom. In the end, the United States, too, abandoned Vietnam to the hands of the Communist killers.

In a speech delivered on 3 February, 1976, Kissinger warned: 'The massive and unprecedented Soviet intervention in the internal affairs of Africa, with military equipment, its advisors, and its transport of 11,000 Cuban forces must be a matter of urgent concern . . . It is the first time that Congress has halted national action in the middle of a crisis . . . If such a precedent is tolerated, we will face harder choices and higher costs in the future.' His challenge was not heeded. The Senate blocked aid to forces which fought for freedom in Angola.

The United States and other major Western powers who

allowed almost half of the world to go to the mass murderers bear the responsibility for rivers of blood. Lord, have mercy upon us!

Let us make restitution for our past sins by helping the Christians who are persecuted by Communists because we and our parents were not watchful.

7: The way ahead

An alternative to detente

'God is light, and in him is no darkness at all' (1 John 1:5). Christ condescended to become a babe wrapped in swaddling clothes, cradled in a manger. Unlike all of us who wish to rise to high position, to assert ourselves by becoming rich and famous, Christ humbled himself.

He humbled himself even more on Good Friday. By becoming a mistreated corpse, he paid the price for our sins and taught us how to die to the world. It is better to resist sin than yield to temptation, but better still to have no reaction at all. A corpse does not react either positively or negatively.

Jesus, who died on Friday, arose on Sunday morning. And while it was dark around him in the grave, he knew that in God there is no darkness. Those who love God cannot remain in dark places; therefore he walked out of the grave.

Those who believe in Christ and follow him unto death will be with him in the resurrection.

Atheism is darkness. It is the absence of God's light in man's mind, whether it be doctrinal atheism or 'a form of godliness' without the power thereof – from God. Let us walk out of the grave of a godless life, as the Lord walked out of darkness.

In Communist countries atheism is forced upon the populace. Even in the free world, Communists spread their godless religion. France, for example, has a very active Union of the Atheists. They wrote: 'Though our fight has a general character, we fight foremost against the Christian religions. Religious people are victims of psychic trouble, nourished and propagated by those who have it in a higher measure.' Thus, according to them, practising Christianity is a 'psychic trouble'.

According to Lenin, 'The non-spatial and non-temporal beings which were invented by the clergy are the products of a diseased mind' (*Materialism and Empirocriticism*). No wonder, then, that Communist governments put Christians in psychiatric asylums.

In Moscow some young Orthodox Christians organised a secret seminary. Its head, Alexander Arghentov, was promptly interned in a hospital for the insane. There Dr Degtiarev, after diagnosing his illness as 'Religiosity', prescribed aminazine, a powerful drug. Now he is in jail.

Well, if the Communists consider Christians madmen, so be it, as long as they have many such madmen in their countries.

Public Opinion and Atheistic Propaganda, a book published in Leningrad, relates that 33 million Soviet citizens declare themselves to be religious believers. There are surely many more who hide their belief for fear of losing their jobs or their liberty. In Leningrad alone, 41 per cent of the people questioned admitted to practising religious ceremonies in their homes. These poor souls were naïve. Cleverer individuals do not answer Soviet polls.

In Soviet Armenia, 70 per cent of the children have been baptised. Infant baptism is such a great risk behind the Iron Curtain that it acquires a value beyond what is known in the free world. It becomes an expression of profound belief.

Our mission's activity has not been in vain. We provide Communist countries with Bibles, Christian books and religious broadcasting, and as a result, their atheist propaganda is blocked. But we are a religious organisation and our only weapon is to lovingly spread the Word of God. Governments, however, have another calling from God than the Church. While the Church is enjoined to bring the wicked to salvation, rulers have been entrusted by God with a sword to punish them. If a state is granted the authority to take action against the murderer of one person, how much greater must be the injunction against Communists who have killed tens of millions.

Therefore, there can be no possibility for detente.

Serghei Uralov, one of the Communist assassins who shot the Russian Emperor and his family, related how Czar Nicholas II on his last day told him, 'I have written a letter to Lenin reminding him that in 1912 his mother asked me to ease the fate of his sister who was deported to Siberia for having spread secret Communist literature. I ordered her freedom and gave her the opportunity to leave the country. Now, in turn, I ask Lenin a favour, not for myself, but for my sick son, that he might be allowed to be with some relatives in the South.' Uralov promised the Emperor that he would forward the petition, but instead shot the whole family that very night. The Empress held the crown prince in her arms and, even after being wounded, prayed to God. She died covering her son's body with her own. The princesses tried to defend themselves with pillows. The Czar received death quietly, in silence.

Kind behaviour to Communists is rewarded only with bullets. A Catholic bishop was in prison in Rhodesia for having defended some guerrillas. The guerrillas thanked him by killing ten Catholic missionaries.

I believe in our work. I know that we can bring Communists, even Communist leaders, to conversion. I believe also in the conversion of gangsters, but I would not recommend any government to leave the solution of its crime problem in the hands of pastors. Police action is necessary. Preaching alone cannot save the world from Communism. A whole complex of political, economic, cultural and military measures are also needed. The Communists have become specialists in psychological warfare, and in order to combat them we must master it ourselves.

Kissinger is incorrect when he says that there is no alternative to detente, that its collapse would mean nuclear war. This is not so. The Soviets make no nuclear war. But neither do they make peace. They have infiltrated high positions in the free world and are cleverer than the children of light. Let us infiltrate the Communist camp with the Gospel.

Everyone behind the Iron Curtain whom we have brought to Christ automatically becomes anti-Soviet and pro-Western because he knows that, whereas in his country religion is oppressed, with us he would be free to worship.

We limit ourselves to our own calling: the preaching of the Gospel. The rulers of the state have their responsibility.

I have been a privileged man. I have been able to speak out for the persecuted and do something for them. In the present book I have spoken in the name of the millions who suffer innocently, but I speak also in the name of the many refugees whose voices are silenced in the free world.

Nguyen Cong Hoan, a Vietnamese politician, and two other members of what used to be the pro-peace opposition in the Saigon Parliament under the Thieu government, escaped from Vietnam by fishing boat and found temporary shelter in Japan.

When Mr Hoan and his colleagues invited the press to a news conference a few weeks after their arrival, they were warned by the police and the office of the United Nations High Commissioners for Refugees that this ran counter to what the Japanese Government expected from them. The police even warned that such a conference might anger the Hanoi government sufficiently to ask for their return, and that it would be difficult to reject such a request.

These Vietnamese refugees, who had left their wives and young children behind to carry out a self-imposed mission of bearing witness, expected both more freedom and greater interest. Now, exiled in a small Japanese town, they were cut off from real contact with those with whom they wished to communicate, and were forced to wait idly for the United States or French embassies to issue them visas. 'I am disappointed,' Mr Hoan said, speaking of the United States. 'I thought the Americans, who were so interested in my country for so long, would have received me more readily.'

Mr Hoan was sadder, as were his friends, over the spiritual aspect of their exile than its material hardships or the uncertainties about their future. They had escaped their country to tell the world of its fate, and either found themselves prevented from giving testimony, or the world unwilling to listen.

'When I first came here [to Japan], I went to watch some other refugees arrive,' said Mr Hoan. 'One was a very old lady. When I asked her why she had come, she fell to her knees and cried, "I pray, do something, speak to the governments, tell them to help us, tell them to help Vietnam." It is the same for me. I want people outside to hear my people. But people are indifferent, not only the Japanese, but even the Vietnamese who have been here for a longer time.

'When I left my country, I had a different idea of what I would do in the outside world. I have had much sadness. I must not let myself be discouraged, although I feel that my hands and feet are tied and I cannot do or say much.'

Mr Hoan is one of millions of refugees from Communist countries.

Learning from the martyrs

Everyone of us can help the martyred church in Communist countries. Even better, we can allow ourselves to be helped by the example of love, of real Christianity, shown by our martyred brethren.

In Red China, a pastor and two Christian girls were sentenced to death. As is common in church history, the persecutors mocked them. The pastor was promised release if he would shoot the girls. He accepted.

When the execution was announced, the girls waited in the prison yard. A fellow prisoner who watched the scene from his cell described their faces as pale but beautiful beyond belief; infinitely sad but sweet. They were fearful, but ready to submit to death without renouncing their faith. Then, flanked by guards, the executioner came with a revolver in his hand: it was their own pastor.

The girls whispered to each other, then bowed respectfully before the pastor. One of them said:

'Before being shot by you, we wish to thank you heartily for what you have meant to us. You baptised us, you taught us the way of eternal life, you gave us Holy Communion with the same hand in which you now hold the gun. May God reward you for all the good you have done us. You also taught us that Christians sometimes commit terrible sins, but that they can be forgiven. When you regret what you are about to do, do not despair like Judas but repent like Peter. God bless you, and remember that our last thought was not one of indignation against your weakness. Everyone passes through hours of darkness. We die with gratitude.'

They bowed again. They knew it was the Lord who had deemed that their suffering should come where they would feel it most: betrayal by their pastor.

The pastor's heart was hardened. He shot the girls, and afterwards was himself shot by the Communists.

The names of the girls were Chiu-Chin-Hsiu and Ho-Hsiu-Tzu. We withhold the pastor's name. This happened in Kiangsi.

Life creates conflicts among men, though not always so dramatic as the one just told. Let us learn from these martyred girls how to meet the betrayal of friendships, or the unfaithfulness of those in whom we have confided.

In another incident in Red China, a girl was cruelly tortured to get her to betray the secrets of the Underground Church. When asked how she could bear so much suffering, she replied, 'It was not hard. My pastor taught me that the real torture lasts a very short time. For each minute of torture, there are ten minutes of looking into enraged faces and at the implements of pain. I kept my eyes closed and since I did not see the stick before it hit me, nor afterwards, the suffering was much reduced. I relied also on Christ's promise: "Blessed are the pure in heart, for they shall see God" (Matt. 5:8). I purified my heart of fear of men, and I learned to see God. So many had seen him before. When the Communists became aware of my defense, they stuck my eyelids open with tape, but it was too late. I had already received a vision of other spheres.'

We can learn from this Christian not to be obsessed by the suffering which faces us, but rather to close our eyes to it. Dead men cannot be afraid. We are meant to be dead to the world, and with hearts purified by the blood of Christ, to look upwards to the heavenly Father.

A book secretly compiled by the true Orthodox Church of the Soviet Union entitled *Give them Peace with the Saints*, has been received in the West. It gives the following accounts:

The first Orthodox priest ever killed by the Communists was John Kotchurov. In Essentuki, priest John Riabuhin, together with many others, had his limbs hacked off and was buried while still breathing. Priest John Krasnov was burned alive. Priest Nikolai Koniuhov, on the other hand, was frozen to death. Priest Alexander Podolskii was beaten to death and those who tried to bury him were shot. The deacon Tikhon sang his own burial service, while his son, aged ten, compelled by the Reds, dug his father's grave. Priest Grigorii Dmitrevskii first had his nose and ears cut off, then his head. Priest Grigorii Nikolski was shot with a bullet through his mouth after saying the liturgy. The murderers told him, 'Now we will give you Holy Communion.'

Anti-Christian terrorism in the Soviet Union has been unceasing for sixty years. Nonetheless, the true Orthodox Church continues to worship God in the underground. I met its archbishop; it was a little like encountering Christ. He began an evening service chanting, 'In the name of the Father and of the Son and of the Holy Ghost,' and immediately the whole congregation was in tears.

For the first time in my life I realised the depth of these words. I recognised myself as the prodigal son who is far removed from the Godhead. I only had his name, just as in prison I had remained with only the names of my wife and son. The reality was unreachable. But I also knew that the one from whom I am so distant is a loving Father who waits for me. His Son sacrificed himself for me. His Spirit draws me.

This archbishop was a man who scarcely needed to preach. The first words of the liturgy did the work.

Let us be helped by these Christians to despise all the difficulties of life, even its horrors, and to remain faithful to the Lord.

Our Japanese, Indian, Swiss, Danish and Brazilian directors have all received threats from Communist terrorists. My son and I work in constant danger of our lives. Christian life and Christian work is not meant to be easy. The Lord said, 'The Son of man *must* suffer,' and we are all sons of man.

In Soviet Lithuania a Christian student, Leonas Sileikis, was brought before a commission of seven teachers to be examined. When asked what she thought about atheist books, she replied, 'They contain lies and slander.' A Communist then delivered a speech against religion and asked her if she would renounce her faith. Her answer was, 'I believe and will continue to do so.' The director of the school explained to her father, who was present, the danger of religion. But the father argued, 'It is not true that religion is dangerous. The fruits of treading religion under your feet are that students no longer respect the teachers; they drink, smoke and whore.' One of the teachers argued, 'Seeing that few go to church nowadays, it is sensible to join the majority.' The father retorted, 'Only corpses flow with the current. A living person can swim against it.' The director warned him, 'With such ideas you will make it impossible for your daughter to continue her studies.' Her father replied, 'It is not I who hinder her, but you. What good is it to study if you have to renounce the highest value, a personal faith?' We do not know yet what happened to the Sileikis family as a result of this interview. But I know about many like them who went to prison.

Leonas Sileikis and her father fulfilled the commandment which I put upon your heart: 'Present your bodies as a living sacrifice, holy, acceptable unto God, which is your reasonable service' (Rom. 12:1).

Learn from heroes, learn from the martyrs.

The gifts are not the same for all

The present book is not a call to action for everyone. Jesus' words are: 'All men cannot receive this saying, save they to whom it is given' (Matt. 19:11).

These words of the Lord Jesus have freed my conscience from many unfounded regrets and much painful remorse. They can free you, too.

It is obvious that not all the commandments in the Bible are written for all believers. Nobody is obliged to fulfill all of them, neither must we feel bad when we cannot accomplish them. Some commandments are given only to the Jewish priests, others only to husbands or wives, others to children. The commandments for masters are not the same as those given to servants. Many verses exclusively concern the generation that conquered Canaan. Some apply only to farmers. God does not expect the same thing from men of various temperaments and different educational backgrounds. Everyone should serve God according to his calling and to his own gift, without torturing his conscience that he cannot do things for which he is not qualified.

In Matthew 19:9 the Lord forbids divorce. It is best to remain till the end with a marriage partner even if he changes your life into hell through repeated betrayals. Perpetual suffering can help develop a Christ-like character; yet the Lord adds immediately that an extreme position of sainthood is not expected of everybody. For those to whom God does not give a special gift, such a commandment is impossible.

In Red China, during the period when the churches were still open, the police broke into a religious service asking for a certain Christian whom they wished to arrest. Desiring to protect him, the believers said there was no one of that name in their congregation, but the one sought came forward and told the police, 'I am the man you seek.' He could not bear a lie, even if prompted by love, and he paid for his integrity with his life.

Such crystalline integrity should be admired, but only in the knowledge that the right attitude towards sainthood is admiration, not imitation. All Christians cannot have the same extreme love for truth. It is a special gift from God.

One cannot smuggle Bibles into the Red camp and do Underground Church work there without using tricks. Whoever says it is possible to do underground work without deception is mistaken. We do not reproach anyone who cannot receive the message of our mission. They have not been given this understanding. Perhaps their calling is different.

A poor Asian Christian with several children read my book *Tortured For Christ*. He immediately sold all he had, which was a modest house, and used it for starting a branch of our mission. He now heads an important Bible-smuggling project for Red China. The saying of Jesus to a rich ruler, 'Sell that thou hast and give to the poor,' cannot be received by all men. It is for those who have received a special grace from God. We can however be inspired by their example and give whatever we can give joyously. God knows that he made us to be different, and he does not expect the same gift from one Christian as from another.

In Lebanon, the Christians fight against Communist-trained and Communist-armed Palestinian guerrillas. In Majdalona, the guerrillas poured gasoline over the furniture in a Christian officer's house, ignited a fuse to trigger a dynamite blast, and fled, believing their work accomplished. Within seconds the officer's sisters would have been killed, but miraculously the fire burning the fuse was quenched – an angel did it.

This occurred in one exceptional case. In countless others Christians died with weapons in their hands attempting to defend their faith. The example of the saints of old who 'turned to flight the armies of the aliens' (Heb. 11:34) is not for all to follow, but only for the Christians who have a special gift.

Not every Christian can bear 'the care of all the church' (2 Cor. 11:28). A world-wide vision is a gift apart. The sorrow engendered for the countries in which Christians are already tortured to death and for other countries which will soon have their own Gulag Archipelago, would break most hearts and drive most men to madness. All these countries experience or will experience severe anti-Christian persecution, and their betrayal by the free world will further hinder the spreading of the Gospel.

We know that betrayal of friendships is a main characteristic of every unregenerated soul. In the case of these countries the free world has gone to an unprecedented extreme.

Just as the average Jew does not wish to hear about Jesus because of the atrocities committed towards his people by men who called themselves Christians, so Cambodians and others will have engraved in their histories: 'Christians, though powerful, abandoned us in the moment of trial and allowed mass-murderers to become rulers; Christians cannot be trusted.'

We do not expect all Christians to share the burden of our vision, but, while doing your own precious work in a narrower sphere and making your own sacrifices, pray for us to whom God has given his charge.

The Gadarenes prayed to Jesus to depart from their coasts (Mark 5:17). They had good reason to do so. He had purged demons from a man by ordering them to enter a herd of swine which then ran down a slope into the sea and drowned. The Gadarenes thus lost their property and food for themselves and their children. How would you have reacted if the entrance of Jesus into your life had meant the loss of your home, your car, your bank account or your job? Perhaps you would continue to use holy phrases but not meaning them. The Gadarenes uttered a prayer which was at least sincere, 'Depart from us, Jesus.'

Jesus is accustomed to being driven out. In Holman Hunt's renowned picture, *The Light of the World*, the Lord is shown begging entrance at a house, his feet turned, not towards the door, but towards the roadway. He has more chance of being refused than accepted, because to accept him costs so dearly.

The apostle Paul writes, 'For Christ Jesus my Lord, I have suffered the loss of all things, and do count them but dung, that I may win Christ' (Phil. 3:8). Do we also look upon our nice furniture, a new car, the better job we just got, the money we possess, as upon repulsive dung? He wished to get away from it – the sooner the better. Is this our attitude towards earthly possessions? Whoever wishes to win Christ must lose them. *Friendship with Jesus is costly. Faith alone saves, but faith does not exist alone. It is always accompanied by great sacrifices for Christ's sake.*

The first revelation of God was given in Hebrew, a language in which the verb 'to have' does not exist. You cannot say in Hebrew, 'I have so much money, I have a house or a car,' because the Hebrews did not 'have' anything. They did not even have the concept of 'having'. *The only possessor of all possessions is God, and you can possess him.* Regarding all other things, you can only be their steward. This is why Christians ask the heavenly Father to give them daily bread. Seemingly, they already have it in a cupboard or the money to buy it, and need not ask for it. But neither the cupboard, the bread, nor the money is theirs. It is God's bread and he can command you not to eat today, but to fast.

You can eat the bread from the cupboard only with his permission.

Preachers who promise prosperity, good health and continual joy if you come to Jesus, lead you astray. On the contrary, you might lose a 'herd of swine'. You are meant to lose all. 'He that forsakes not *all* that he has, cannot be my disciple,' says the Lord (Luke 14:33). Because of this, the real prayer of most people is not what they speak with their lips, but, 'Depart from us, Jesus.' Happily this is not the prayer of all.

In Lebanon, Christians are killed by Communist-indoctrinated and armed Palestinians, but God's true children do not lose their lives by bullets. They have already lost them at the moment of their conversion. Their lives are no longer their own.

I share with you a letter found on the body of a Lebanese Christian student aged twenty-two, who was shot while peacefully on his way to Nabha to share Christmas with his family there.

'If my foreboding is fulfilled that I will be killed on this way, I tell my mother and my family: Do not be sad, do not weep exceedingly. My absence will be short and we will see each other in heaven. There joy reigns. Do not fear. God's mercy will reunite us. I have only one request. Forgive from all your heart those who have killed me. Pray with me that my blood, though it is that of a sinner, might be accepted for the sins of Lebanon, that it might be accepted together with the blood of the victims of all religions . . . May my death teach men love . . . Pray and pray and love your enemies. If Abou-Khalil can give some of his planks for a coffin, I will lie very well in it. Please, make no burial meal. May men forgive me. I am dust. I, a sinner, in Jesus Christ, Ghasibe Kayrouz.'

I am a Jew and feel proud to have such an Arab as my brother in Christ. When he accepted Jesus, he had lost everything, even the desire to live on earth one more day than God ordained. He lost all enmity towards those who might take his life. Forgiving his murderers was as easy for him as breathing.

No one will ever be able to describe all the misdeeds of Communism. Solzhenitsyn described some, but not all. Edward Buca, a former inmate of Soviet concentration camps, recounted in his book, *Vorkuta*, how a Communist police officer had tortured a woman by pushing a large candle into her vagina and lighting it. He told her, 'You have a little time to think things over. Soon the flame will reach your body. When you're ready to sign the confession, signal by blinking three times.' The flame burned down to her body while the officer looked on calmly. Once he removed the candle, lit a cigarette with it and put it back.

Prisoners who tried to escape were savagely beaten, then tied behind galloping reindeer and dragged to death. One prisoner was compelled to play the harmonica while the corpses were exposed to public view.

Soviet Christians have no lives of their own to lose. Like the ancient Hebrews, they do not even have the notion of having. From the hell of Soviet prisons, a believer smuggled out the following letter, which shows a heart full of peace and adoration, seemingly unaware of the horrors surrounding it.

'"Marvellous are thy works" (Ps. 139:14). I greet and congratulate you with these words, dear mother and dear daughter, on your birthday. This was the text of the first cable in the world in 1845 – a verse from the Bible. The inventor of the telegraph was Samuel Morse. It is significant that his father, George Morse, was a renowned evangelist. This text was written 3,000 years ago and entered so deeply into the hearts of many generations of men with a living faith in God, that for 2,500 years it was faultlessly transcribed by hand. In 1455, it was first printed. The first printed book was the Bible.

'The works of God are truly marvellous in all things, in nature and technique, in the lives of all men, in the destiny of people and of mankind, and specially of his Church. It is a great joy to contemplate the work of His hand and of His creative mind in all that surrounds us. The Bible is also the first book from which men read when circling around the moon . . .

'I see from your letters that you are very troubled because of me. My beloved, this should not be. Keep your health, do not let your heart be troubled. May it be in perfect peace, because everything happens according to his will.'

Such Christians see God's will and God's good intentions

even while bearing Communist atrocities, whereas unbelieving men or those who believe superficially, say to
Jesus, 'Depart from us; you made us lose a herd of swine.'

Gratitude for suffering

We do not have the right notion of might. 'Might' to us
means the power to crush, subdue, suppress or to punish.
But there is another kind of might: this is 'the might to
love', to be patient and quiet, to suffer innocently and to
return good to the wrongdoer. When we think about
energy, we usually conceive of it as kinetic, a quality which
makes all things move. There also exists the huge reservoir
of potential energy, or energy at rest. This is the power of
quietness, of serenity.

A Communist officer told a Christian while beating him:
'I am almighty, as you suppose your God to be. I can kill
you.' The Christian answered: 'The real power is all on my
side, for I can love you while you torture me to death.' Such
is God's almightiness – it is reflected in the deep tranquil-
lity of the souls of saints. They do not ask the troublesome
question, 'Why all the sorrow?' because they have learned
to love the cross, and to be rejected without comfort. Once
you take this attitude, the perplexity ceases. What child is
troubled when he receives a much-desired gift?

The peak of holiness is never to ask anything for yourself,
never to refuse a cross with which God honours you, and to
accept life humbly as it comes, without questions. We are
not ready to understand the answers yet. Some day we will
know as also we are known by God (1 Cor. 13:12). A saint
is not a man who possesses a great light from God. He
possesses nothing. He *is* a nothing through whom shines
God's power to endure, to hope, and to love even the worst
of his fellow men. Who knows if the murderer of today will
not become a future apostle; if today's loose woman will not
be a Magdalene? And can God, who is almighty, not
compensate in eternity any wrongs suffered here for a little
while?

We bless the Father, the Son and the Holy Ghost. We say
to the Lord, 'Blessed is the womb that bore thee' (Luke
11:27), and we advance on the path of faith without tor-

menting ourselves with many 'whys' about suffering, which we welcome, because through suffering we can joyfully glorify Christ.

George Vins, the general secretary of the only faithful Baptist Union in the Soviets, was in prison. His mother wrote to him: 'The day after tomorrow will be the anniversary of your imprisonment. Really a sad anniversary. But be strong, my child. You act with nobility, as a worthy son of your father. [George Vins' father died in jail for his Christian witness.] May the Lord shed his light on you, and lift all the burden from your heart. May God keep you. May He preserve your soul from evil and from hardening amidst the sorrows which confront you. I pray unceasingly that they may pity you. Let us abandon ourselves to Him, because the breath of our life is in His hands. He knows how exhausted we are and that we have no respite while bearing our cross. When he comes, he will free us from our burden. The time of blessedness is near. The Lord comes. Formerly, your father sang such words with me. Now I sing them with you, and in eternity we will sing them all three. I embrace you and greet all the children of the Father. Your mother: Lydia Vins.'

The Baptist pastor Pavel Vasilievitch died in a concentration camp. His wife, sentenced to ten years, wrote a letter to him five years after his death, believing him still alive: 'I know that we will see each other after death where there is no sorrow nor separation, where happiness and peace wait for us. I know that we did not meet on earth accidentally, that the Lord himself united us in love and marriage. He reserved for us a hard way compared to our strength. I thank God for all our life together, for all the sufferings, for His love and grace towards us. May God bless you while you walk before him.'

Suffering torments some souls, drives them to despair, even to suicide. Others are grateful for it. I have seen faithful Christian prisoners dancing for joy. They have recognised God as almighty, and in patience they show love toward the evil men who torture them. They know that God's love is irresistible. It will conquer.

Speak in this manner and act with love and patience yourself when you are wronged. Being of one spirit with the

155

Father, you will understand his ways better, and your doubts will cease.

Try to do some practical good instead of criticising God for not doing what you consider best. Learn from the martyrs.

We received a letter from the mother of Baptist prisoner Valerii Nasaruk. She writes, 'My son wished to come to the West and learn to be a preacher. God said, "No. I lead you into another school, in prison." I attended his trial. It was hard on me. I would have preferred to be in his place. But God gives one power to bear everything. The greatest trial was when they asked me in court – I, his mother – to advise Valerii to change his ways. I could not do it. I comforted him. The world accuses us, his parents, for his being sentenced, saying it is the result of our teaching. Even some believers cannot understand us. But neither was our Saviour understood. Peter warned him about saving his own life. We are allowed to visit Valerii. Thank God he is courageous. He greets you all.'

Valerii is courageous in prison. His mother, deprived of her son and condemned by many, is able, through Christ, not to be depressed. Do you see now how wrong it is for you to be depressed? Learn from the heroism of the persecuted Christians.

In Russia, a monk passed by some soldiers who were learning to shoot. Their target was a cross. The Christian called to them, 'I will not allow you to shoot at this symbol.' They laughed at him and shouted back, 'How can you stop us from doing what we like?' The monk quietly placed himself before the cross saying, 'You will have to shoot at me.' One soldier did; he missed. The others put down their guns.

The Christian Varvara was a nurse in a prison. She was so good that a murderer of seven people, who lay dying in the ward, asked her, 'Are you an angel or a human? How can you be so kind to me?' She replied, 'Because you suffer.' 'I deserve it,' he confessed, 'I have killed many.' Comforting him, she said, 'God is gracious. Those who have sinned but little do not need great pity. For great sinners, he has much grace. For you he has grace beyond grace. You are more valuable in his eyes than all the rest.' The criminal was greatly moved. 'How can God take you and me to the same heaven?' he asked. 'Is he blind? Does he not see the difference between us?' Then Sister Varvara began to weep. The man was awestruck. 'You weep for me? Except for my mother when I was a child, nobody has ever wept for me.' Then he begged her, 'Pray.' This sinner had an Orthodox background, and she, an Evangelical, prayed with him in the Orthodox manner, knowing that only this could touch his heart. He died repenting.

Learn from the martyred brethren a new type of Christianity: Christianity as Christ meant it to be.

Be a co-martyr

Not everyone is called to be a martyr, but by sharing with them we become co-martyrs. There are saints living today who follow in the footsteps of the martyrs of old like St Ignace of Antioch, in the second century, who, when sentenced to be thrown to the wild beasts, wrote: 'I rejoice because of the beasts prepared for me, and I pray that they may be ferocious against me. I will provoke them to swallow me at once and not to be shy, as has sometimes happened . . . I know what is good for me. Only now I begin to be a disciple . . . I am facing death. Forgive me, brethren. Do not prevent me from gaining life.'

Bonhoeffer, who died a martyr's death under the Nazis in Germany, once wrote: 'The hungry need bread. To allow the hungry to remain hungry would be a blasphemy against God and one's neighbour . . . If the hungry do not attain to faith, then the fault lies with those who refuse the bread. To provide the hungry with bread is to prepare the way for the coming of grace.'

People are hungry not only for food, but also for the Word of God. A quarter of a million people are born every day, mostly in countries where the Gospel is unknown or is not free.

Families of Christian martyrs lack a piece of bread. Will you be a blasphemer against God through not caring? Or do you wish to help?

Do you wish also to be helped by them? Then change

your attitudes in life according to the examples of our martyred brethren.

A Christmas letter was smuggled out of the Soviet Union and arrived in the West after much delay. It was written by Christian writer Alexander Petrov-Agatov, who spent a total of thirty years in prisons and concentration camps for his faith. The letter is a gem of love:

On Christmas Eve I remember all men, independent of their faith and colour, of their social position or level of education. I remember men in power and those who suffer in jails and camps, the rich and the poor, the strong and the weak, those who have risen to peaks and those who have fallen into the abyss, the sick and the healthy, the persecuted and the persecutors. Foremost, I think about those whom I left only recently after having been with them in prison and camps for almost thirty years . . . On our festive table there is a small Christmas tree, apples, grapes, and other dainties. In my heart words ring like a bell: Can you eat all these things while at least one man is hungry? Can you sleep in a warm bed, when somewhere a prisoner is not allowed to lie down even on the cold concrete?

Garlands ornament my Christmas tree while the heavy chains of slavery and barbed wire surround the camps. I do not write only about Soviet camps and prisons; I think also about all those who do not eat and drink this night, who cannot look at the sparkling star which made Christ known to the wise men because the prison windows are covered with planks.

I greet, on Christmas day, our eagles and doves – mothers and wives, brides and those who could not become brides – my sisters who take the cross for the word of God, for truth, for righteousness, for faithfulness towards God and love towards men . . .

Christmas greetings to all the persecuted, the suffering, to all those who seek light. Christmas greeting to all persecutors and oppressors, to all those who curse and confiscate.

Christmas greetings to the person who betrayed me seven years ago. I visited the church in which you were a leader. I wished to see you face to face, but was told that you do not work any more. But do you ever pray? Pray, pray.

All men, prisoners and guards, men of the secret police and patrol officers, secretaries of the Communist central committees and presidents – pray while it is not too late. There will be no second birth of Christ. There will be a second coming. 'Behold, I come soon,' says the Lord. Soon, very soon.

Or take as your teacher in faith sister Nijole Sadunaite who, tried for her Christian activity in Soviet Lithuania, said before the court:

Truth needs no defense, because it is all powerful and unconquerable. Only deceit and lies, being powerless before truth, need weapons, soldiers and prisons to prolong their infamous rule. A partial government digs its own grave. I am on the right side and am ready to lose liberty for truth. I will even gladly give my life. Only those who love have the right to blame and criticise the objects of their love. Therefore I speak to you. You rejoice about your victory. Victory over what? Over morality? . . . Over mean and debased men, infected by fear? . . . Thanks to God, not all men have compromised yet. We [Christians] are not many in society, but quality is on our side. Without fearing prison, we must condemn all actions which lead to injustice and humiliation. We must distinguish what is written by men from what is commanded by God. We owe to Caesar only what remains after having given to God what is his due. The most important thing in life is to free the heart and mind from fear, because yielding to evil is the greatest sin.

This is the happiest day of my life. I am tried for the cause of truth and love towards men. What cause could be more important? I have an enviable fate, a glorious destiny. My condemnation will be my triumph. I regret only having done so little for men. Standing today on the side of the eternal Truth, of Jesus Christ, I remember his fourth beatitude, 'Blessed are they which do hunger and thirst after righteousness, for they shall be filled' (Matt. 5:6).

How could I not rejoice when God almighty has promised that light will overcome darkness and truth will overcome error and lies? May God give us the assurance that his last judgment will be favourable to all of us. I will ask this in prayer for you every day of my life. Let us love each other and we will be happy. Only the one who does not love is unhappy. We must condemn evil, but we must love the man, even the one in error. This you can learn only at the school of Jesus Christ, who is the only truth for all, the only way and the only life. Good Jesus, your Kingdom come into our souls.

Sister Sadunaite was sentenced to three years in prison, and thus she was ordained as an example for the universal Church.

Our mission is not only a channel for conveying help to Christians far away in foreign lands, but, through our martyred brethren, is also a source of light and blessing for Christians in the Western world.

Hands which have worn chains can bless well. Receive the benedictions of those who suffer for the holy cause.

For correspondence with the author, inquiries and gifts for the underground church, the addresses are:

Christian Mission to the Communist World
POB 19
Bromley Kent BR1 1DY
Britain

Jesus to the Communist World
PB598 Penrith NSW 2750
Australia

Voice of the Martyrs
POB 476
Agege-Lagos
Nigeria

Love in Action
POB 4532
11–31 Green Park
New Delhi
India

INQUIRIES & GIFTS MAYBE SENT TO:
JESUS TO THE COMMUNIST WORLD INC.
P O BOX 117, PORT CREDIT
MISSISSAUGA, ONT.   L5G 4L5

Ellerslie
Auckland 5
New Zealand

Torrance 90509
California
USA